PACIFIC EDGE

CONTEMPORARY ARCHITECTURE ON THE PACIFIC RIM

Peter Zellner

with essays by
Aaron Betsky
Davina Jackson
Akira Suzuki

RIZZOLI
NEW YORK

CONTENTS

For my Parents, Yolanda and Peter Sr

ACKNOWLEDGMENTS

This book was completed in no small part due to the support,
kind advice and continued goodwill of the following individuals.
To them I say thank you!

Aaron Betsky, Ingrid Cranfield, Neil M. Denari, Lucas Dietrich,
Heidi Dokulil, Jordi Farrando, Richard Gilmore, Aaron Hayden,
Sand Helsel, Davina Jackson, Moriko Kira, Darko Kramer, Adriana Leon,
Andew Liang, Laurence Liauw, cj Lim, Nopadol Limwantakul, Carey Lyon,
Yves Nacher, Laurel Porcari, Eul-Ho Suh, Sonny Sutanto, Akira Suzuki,
Manuel Tardits, Noriko Takiguchi, Stephen Varady, Ang Gin Wah,
Mary Wall and Mirko Zardini.

First published in the United States of America in 1998 by
RIZZOLI INTERNATIONAL PUBLICATIONS, INC.
300 Park Avenue South, New York, NY 10010

Copyright © 1998 by Thames and Hudson Ltd, London
Texts copyright © 1998 by Peter Zellner
Essays copyright © 1998 by the individual authors

HALF-TITLE PAGE O'Connell house by Architecture Warren & Mahoney
TITLE PAGE McWilliam Residence by Clare Design

INTRODUCTION
SURFACE CROSSINGS AND EDGE ENVIRONMENTS

Give or take an inlet here or there, the Pacific Ocean covers some 165,384,000 square kilometres of continuous water surface. Its edges lap on to the shores of nearly thirty-five countries and it encompasses East Asian, Polynesian, American, Melanesian, South-east Asian, Latin American and Australasian cultures. The Asia-Pacific region, popularly referred to as the Pacific Rim or the Pacific Basin, is home to some of the fastest developing economies on the planet and as a result some of the world's fastest growing cities. For instance, the frontier towns of China's southern 'special enterprise zones' are growing at dizzying rates into urban agglomerations, which may hold as many as thirty million people by mid-century. Shenzhen, one such city, was not conceived of until the mid-1980s but it is already bigger than Seattle or Melbourne. South-east Asian countries, Singapore in particular, are marvels of contemporary social advancement and technological development. In many Asian countries a massive middle class is emerging. By the

Thus this mysterious divine Pacific zones the whole world's bulk around it; makes all coasts one bay to it; seems the tide-beating heart of the earth. Herman Melville, *Moby Dick*

close of this decade some seventy-five million households in Asia, not even counting those in Japan, will have incomes comparable to those of most families in the United States. Admittedly, many of the economies of this region are currently experiencing the souring effects of a financial downturn and this 'adjustment' may temporarily check urban growth in the region. But in the long run the continued, runaway growth of the Asia-Pacific region's newest urban agglomerations seems inevitable.

CLARE DESIGN SKI AND SKURF

In the Asian-Pacific context, architecture has become a sort of pawn in the complex game of financial exchange and rapid urban growth. More often than not, the impetus for the architecture is pure financial incentive. Rarely are cultural or social needs uppermost. The cities of the Asia-Pacific region are beginning to exhibit a stultifying sameness; an endless urban reproduction in Santiago, as in Sydney, as in Seoul, of the same malls, airports, hotels and housing developments. The need to make and express cultural difference and social vitality through built form seems, at times, woefully undervalued by the political and financial bodies that are driving the region's development. However, there is also a loose matrix of architects and designers that is starting to develop around the production of a specific and vital 'new world' architectural agenda. Between Malaysia and Mexico, Australia and Alaska, Latin America and East Asia, there are architects who are dedicated to, and have been thinking about, a locally oriented reading of architecture that also confidently operates within a larger global context. Some of these architects are quite well established and celebrated while others are relatively young and unknown.

With its voracious vitality, history robs architecture of its meaning and endows it with new meaning.
Umberto Eco, *Travels in Hyperreality*

What they share, across cultures and across the Pacific, is a dedication to the production of buildings and ideas for buildings that are specific to their cultural place and geographic position. This book presents the work of some of those architects and explores the ways in which architectural creativity throughout the Asia-Pacific region can be exchanged, shared and celebrated.

The *Los Angeles Times* recently reported an extraordinary, if somewhat bizarre development. Orange County architects, many of them victims of the early 1990s downturn in the southern Californian real-estate market, have found new prosperity and employment designing 'California-Spanish' housing tracts and 'Irvine-style'

TOYO ITO YATSUSHIRO
FIRE STATION

master-planned communities in Jakarta, Indonesia. Architects from firms based in Newport Beach and Costa Mesa are supervising the construction of beige-and-pink, Spanish-tiled housing estates with names like 'the Riverside Golf Club and Residential Community' and 'Balboa Island' – some fourteen thousand kilometres south-west of Los Angeles. Complete with gated entrances, bicycle trails and outdoor sculptures, and planned to recreate what the urban theorist Mike Davis would surely deem the ersatz and venal 'designer Mission style' of the Californian dream, these housing developments could easily be at home anywhere in the south-west of the United States – except for the fact that they are being laid out in the midst of rice paddies and ancient ritual burial sites. Driven by the desires of the newly affluent Indonesian middle classes for all things Western, Jakarta's developers have banked on the 'southern Californian look' as they've seen it along the Newport Beach coastline or, more likely, on such television programmes as 'Baywatch' and 'Melrose Place'. While we could decry this phenomenon as yet another example of the loss of traditional, localized cultures to the banal sway of American television and a sad demonstration of the 'biscuit-cutter logic' at work in the contemporary city, it does reveal a lot about the possibilities (or for that matter dangers) of transcultural exchange on an urban scale. The Pacific Ocean has become a space across which cultural and economic signals – such as architecture – are being transferred and consumed with increasing speed. Indeed, as artificial structures like the World Wide Web and the global financial market accelerate and intensify the exchange of

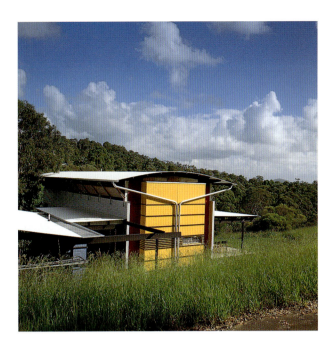

CLARE DESIGN CLARE RESIDENCE

resources and ideas, the vast geographical and cultural distances between places like Orange County, California, and Jakarta, Indonesia, begin to seem insignificant. For

We are in this strange tension where the global and local are very strong. We don't work any more clearly within any kind of continuity but we don't work either in an extreme, isolated new space. [We are] in a period of time characterized by the coexistence of different realities, we are often constrained to act in the margins. This is exactly the place where these realities meet. Josep Lluis Mateo

better or worse, the dynamic rhythms of the media have established patterns of communication that have cut us loose from the restrictions we once knew. As a consequence, the seamless transfer of a faux 'Californian-Colonial style' to the 'fast cities' of South-east Asia over the Pacific Ocean suggests that architecture is no longer valued for its ability to mark time, place or local tradition – it has been sucked headlong into the stream of cultural signals that are being zapped from one far-flung locale to another. Architecture, or built social form, has become a vital commodity in the phenomenal and risky dance of delocalized social interchange that people everywhere seem intent on pursuing. The vital, even fragile identities of locale and community, the very things that help to distinguish one place from the next, are in real danger of being consumed by monolithic and omnipresent transnational capital movements and media barters. Our cities, in particular those in the rapidly developing nations of the Asia-Pacific region, may end up like the 'corporate arcologies', the city-sized megalithic buildings described in William Gibson's cyberpunk novel *Neuromancer* – dominated by corporate global conglomerates, cities of bland greyness, 'the colour of television, tuned to a dead channel'.

The world has changed. We participate in the evolution of a global network, both real and electromagnetic, in which every point seems to hold equal valency, each location is equally accessible and hence equally valued in the global mark-up of place. No place becomes more or less important than any other. We are all, more or less, one keytap away from each other. In architectural or urbanistic terms, this widespread togetherness tends to lead to the rapid and uncritical translation of city and building types from one community to another. In the afterglow of the atomic century this presages a cultural misadventure of enormous and unprecedented proportions. However, if we accept that the macroeconomic concept of an 'Asia-Pacific Rim' has become a reality, then perhaps we may start to find ways in which such collapsed 'boundary conditions' could reveal opportunities for the making of new cities and architectures on a microeconomic scale. The overused aphorism 'think globally, act locally' must work in this instance because, as Mateo has pointed out, local, specific and critically regional cultures still, paradoxically, bear relevance for us despite the increasing dissolution of national boundaries. Local cultures do not become less important or less necessary in the context of global communication: just different, more interesting and potentially much more vital.

Consider the generally Japanese spatial sensibility evident in the works of Pacific West Coast architects such as Charles Eames or Franklin Israel, the tantalizing imprint of Louis Kahn's work in Tadao Ando's architecture or Australian Glenn Murcutt's long-avowed interest in the Californian Case Study houses of Pierre Koenig and Craig Ellwood. Clearly, communication, exchange and reinterpretation across the Pacific have already produced moments of significant, critical and worthy transregional architectures. Fastidious crafters of form and space, these architects have carefully woven unfamiliar or foreign ideas and spatial types into a local idiom

MILLER HULL ISLAND CABIN

and climate, creating new architectures out of their appreciation for native and extraneous traditions. Their architecture convinces, both at the regional level and in the larger global context. Such successful examples indicate that there are options other than the dominant-centre/dependent-periphery model of cultural communication available to architects. Yet today, in a world in which the idea of centre and periphery really seem irrelevant, making the effort to respond to place or context seems unnecessary when it is so much easier to download the latest consumer global trend for reproduction at home. In opposition to this trend of increasing architectural or cultural sameness this book will demonstrate that architects working in the Asia-Pacific region are deeply concerned to make an architecture that addresses its immediate location and cultural situation as well as the possibilities of the larger international dialogue. The architects featured here are mining a new vitality of place out of difference and variation and, from their positions on the global urban landscape, they are beginning to remap the specific on to the general. Study the fabulously light and delicate architecture of the Clares on Australia's Sunshine Coast or Glenda Kapstein's massive and substantial buildings in Chile and one will find an architecture of careful dimension and ample substance. Compare the highly synthesized and refined works of Toyo Ito and Neil M. Denari against Ushida Findlay's flowing spaces and sinuous forms or the complex and street-smart buildings of Eric Owen Moss and one will find architects creating buildings of great difference but equally convincing outcome within the same cities and the same cultures. Contemplate TAX's taut and angular forms in and around Mexico City or Kyu Sung Woo's careful geometries and tight compositions in Seoul and

TAX HOUSE IN VALLE DE BRAVO

Critical Regionalism tends to flourish in those cultural interstices which in one way or another are able to escape the optimizing thrust of universal civilization. Its appearance suggests that the received notion of dominant cultural centre surrounded by dependent, dominated satellites is ultimately an inadequate model by which to assess the present state of modern architecture.

Kenneth Frampton, *Modern Architecture: A Critical History*

one discovers that these architects share similar attitudes towards assembly, site planning and materiality, if not similar cultural agendas. Indeed, to reflect on the various architects, locations and projects featured in this book is to understand that Asian-Pacific architectures are almost too complex to classify, too diverse to analyze, yet strong enough to resist and overcome the temptations of bland repetition. What the architectures of the region do share, however, is the actuality of a social project capable of remaking the general and nebulous into the specific and distinct. Like the

NEIL M. DENARI TOKYO HI-RISE

Global Positioning System (GPS) satellites that orbit our planet, allowing hikers, farmers, jet pilots and sailors to know their exact location on the globe within tens of metres, these multiregional architectures can act as critical, localizing social technologies – as ways and means of pinpointing the local within the global and inscribing the global within the local.

BUILDING REGIONAL DIFFERENCE

In an age of hyperaccelerated development and mediated communication it is increasingly necessary for Asian-Pacific architectural cultures to remain meaningfully regional. The bridging and testing of differences will promote intelligent examination and sharing of valid architectural concepts and at the same time obviate the danger of producing insensitive or stereotypical projects and buildings. This book asks the reader to think of the Asia-Pacific region not so much as a seamless continuum but as an energetic, multilayered matrix of vital cultures and places engaged in both the preservation of local identity and the exchange of new ideas and possibilities. By collecting works of thirty-three architects from around and within the region, this publication compares and contrasts various architectural intents and outcomes. In the process *Pacific Edge* attempts to demonstrate how intelligent and self-aware architectural ideas may flow between one part of the Asia-Pacific region and another. It does not, however, seek to be a pattern book or a set of instructions for producing new Asian-Pacific architectures. Architects should operate with the idea of cross-pollination in mind but should avoid giving encouragement to the growth of the neutered, corporatized world exemplified by the consumer-ready, housing-tract developments that are being constructed in such numbers. If architects are to play a significant role in the future of their cities, they must meet head-on the challenge of interchange and hybridization. The reward will be controlled, fascinating moments of cultural and architectural oscillation and feedback and ultimately vital, self-aware and generous new architectures and city forms.

MORPHOSIS SUN TOWER

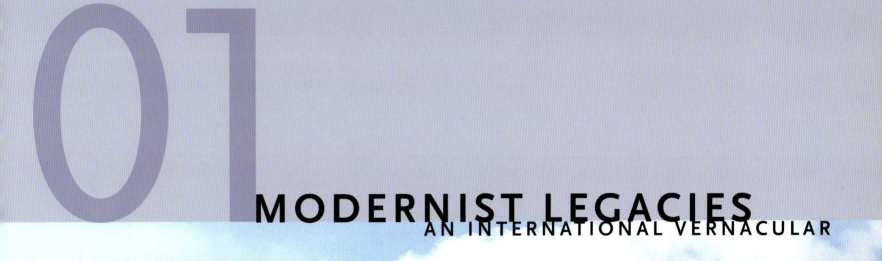

01
MODERNIST LEGACIES
AN INTERNATIONAL VERNACULAR

International Modernism, a product primarily of European thinking and secondarily, some may say, of clever American packaging, developed as an architectural response to the challenges of twentieth-century industrialization and technological advancement and to the problems associated with rapid urban development in the Western world. However, this architecture was to have a wide effect all over the globe, in particular in the developing cities of the New World. In their book, *The International Style* (1932), Henry Russell Hitchcock and Phillip Johnson established a guidebook of sorts to the formal and visual principles of the new architecture. This was an unadorned architecture, stripped of the stylistic excesses of the nineteenth century and tooled into an abstract, crisp

In contrast to the legend of a seamless, unified and inevitable 'International Style', the picture that emerges from the 1930s is one of dissemination in which newly invented paradigms possessing an aura of Modernity and universality were simultaneously extended and criticized ... while the new architecture encountered fierce opposition and rejection in some quarters, it was welcomed and adopted as an appropriate basis for cultural expression in others ... Despite the checks of political reaction and traditionalism, modern architecture established itself on widespread foundations. In effect this was a new tradition with several intellectual and territorial strands, which would continue to be developed and transformed in the post-war world.

William J. R. Curtis, *Modern Architecture since 1900*

and functional machine aesthetic. This architecture was efficient and hence morally appropriate for those cities seeking to streamline themselves (and their citizens) for twentieth-century life. Indeed, the book and the accompanying exhibition at the Museum of Modern Art in New York championed Utopian, functionalist visions and projects that displayed the possibilities of life in a new century; the dream of a Universal Modern existence crossing all cultures and all cultural spaces. This International Style, although intended as a description and not a prescription, must have seemed less than partial to the needs of different locales or cultures. Instead it stood for progress and for the most part a Western or European definition of twentieth-century values. But by mid-century, Modern architecture, once adapted to various locales across the globe, had inevitably begun to diverge and split away from the purist, universally applicable, volumetrically regular standards of the International Style. During the mid-1950s, architects such as Alvar Aalto, Oscar Niemeyer and even Le Corbusier – perhaps the earliest proponent of a universal architecture – were pursuing personal, expressive and often regional interpretations of the Modernist precept. In other words, Modernism had become less a set of rules to be slavishly followed than an underlay or palimpsest, which could be overwritten to suit the specific needs of a project or place. Across the Asia-Pacific Rim, a region which developed dramatically after the close of the Second World War, the International Style was intelligently adapted to suit the geographical, climatic and cultural needs of places as varied as Mexico City, Los Angeles or Tokyo. Architects such as Harry Seidler or Robin Boyd in Australia, Luis Barragán and Juan O'Gorman in Mexico, Kenzo Tange and Kunio Maekawa in Japan or Richard Neutra and Charles Eames on the West Coast of the United States demonstrated that mid-century Modernity could be understood as a kind of new international vernacular – a tautological architecture that was both here and there, specific and general.

Today, many architects around the Asia-Pacific Rim are continuing to explore and develop the possibilities of a Modern architecture tailored to the local context. In Osaka, Waro Kishi has adjusted the Miesian tendency for a limited and minimalist use of materials to the Japanese tradition of expressively detailing connections and gaps, creating a true tension between the singular force of Mies's reductive palette and the potential richness of the Japanese context. Singaporean architect Ang Gin Wah is building projects that search out the meaning of global modernity in an age of increasingly specific cultural complexity in South-east Asia. His Wong House, a juxtaposition of a floating, shade-delivering tropical, 'butterfly roof' and a high Modernist pavilion, achieves a unique and pleasing level of cultural hybridization. While in Chile the Modern movement was never as easily assimilated as in Brazil or Mexico, Mathias Klotz has designed a series of small to medium-sized houses that are both reductive structures and seemingly poetic nautical hymns from the faraway shores of his Andean country to the early works of a Le Corbusier or a Marcel Breuer. In Tokyo, Mikan, a youthful collaborative formed of four separate ateliers, is creating a set of late modern works that range from the cool to the playful and that fuse disparate influences to challenge the modern orthodoxy. Daniel Alvarez and Alberto Kalach of TAX (Taller Arquitectura X) draw on the heritage of Mexican master Luis Barragán and the legacy of Louis Kahn, combining the former's love of spatial rhythm with the latter's sense of mass and austerity. In his designs for a Sydney apartment and a small urban extension, Australian Stephen Varady explores the modern interest in kinetics and his own interest in Kazimir Malevich's tektons to develop a series of spaces and surfaces, which reflect the Modernist project's concern with form and movement.

What these architects' works collectively suggest is that International Modernism, once reviled for its universalizing and, perhaps, culturally anaesthetizing tendencies, is now wholly integrated into various local societies and in due course has returned to the global scene in new and unexpected forms. While these architects may share an interest in the pioneering efforts of Le Corbusier, Kahn and Mies, their works are marked by a sense of culturally adaptive vigour. If their architectural ideas come largely from the Modernist catalogue, their efforts are always directed towards merging that universal idiom with locale, custom or technique. Their buildings clearly suggest that being part of a global movement is not in complete opposition to the act of embracing and extending a distinct and local cultural heritage.

WARO KISHI
KYOTO, JAPAN

*Building connections
between Modernist
reductivism and
the Japanese space-
making tradition*

HOUSE IN HIGASHI-OSAKA

Carefully composed twin
3.6-metre-wide frontage modules
set this house apart from its
suburban setting.

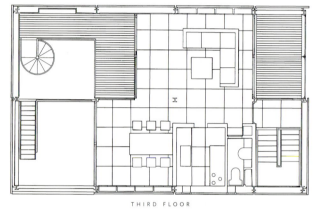

THIRD FLOOR

JAPANESE ARCHITECT Waro Kishi is a virtuoso, if prudent,
practitioner of a revisited and reflective Modernist architecture.
Kishi has been widely praised for his sensitive and restrained
buildings. His works seem to echo Mies van der Rohe's
minimalist use of materials and reductive palette and yet to
register the rich ancient Japanese tradition of expressive and
beautiful detailing of connections and gaps, often creating a
true tension between these two architectural forces. In many
instances, Kishi goes beyond Mies in pursuing a truly

HOUSE IN HIGASHI-OSAKA

The third-floor living-dining area
is partly covered with a semi-
transparent roof creating a gradual
transition between the house's
internal spaces and its vertical
courtyard.

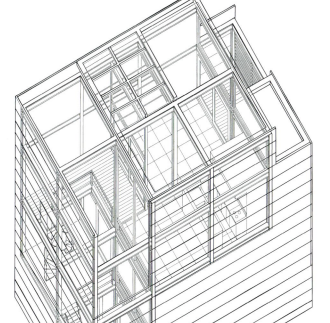

AXONOMETRIC VIEW

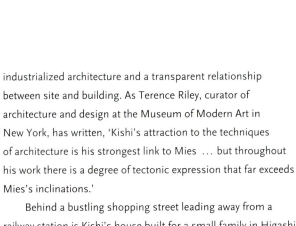

HOUSE IN HIGASHI-OSAKA

The highly structured vertical
courtyard is open to the sky
and filled by a tree.

industrialized architecture and a transparent relationship
between site and building. As Terence Riley, curator of
architecture and design at the Museum of Modern Art in
New York, has written, 'Kishi's attraction to the techniques
of architecture is his strongest link to Mies … but throughout
his work there is a degree of tectonic expression that far exceeds
Mies's inclinations.'

Behind a bustling shopping street leading away from a
railway station is Kishi's house built for a small family in Higashi
Osaka, which thoughtfully retraces early Modernist investigations
into the architectural applications of industrial technologies
and uniform building products. But if the early modern usage
of industrialized materials was deeply political and heroic in
intent, here Kishi uses easily available, prefabricated and
decidedly 'unheroic' materials, yet in an original, poetic fashion.
This small house tests and transforms mainstream Japanese
construction methods and materials into an elevated reading of
the metropolitan condition. Kishi's Memorial Hall in Yamaguchi,
completed to commemorate the fiftieth anniversary of the

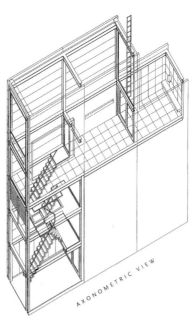

AXONOMETRIC VIEW

HOUSE IN NIHONBASHI

This house is built on an extremely small plot of land in downtown Osaka. The plot for the house is so narrow that its façade, only 2.5 metres wide, fills the site's entire street frontage.

HOUSE IN NIHONBASHI

The 6-metre-high dining room caps the house with an expansive light-filled space removed from the din of Osaka's bustling city centre.

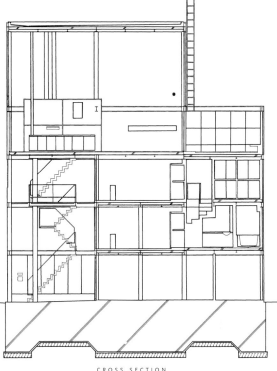

foundation of the medical faculty of Yamagata University, acts as a venue for alumni gatherings, discussions of leading-edge research and for conferences, meetings, seminars and lectures. Students, faculty and visitors relax in the hall's ground-floor lounge, which faces out towards a pond in a garden corner of the campus. In this project, Kishi merges the garden and building into an entity that recalls the Modernist dissolution of spatial boundaries by means of a rigorously applied, free-span, steel-framed, glass-skinned architecture. Kishi's project for a house in Nihonbashi is built on an extremely small plot of land in downtown Osaka. The plot for the house is so narrow that its façade, two and a half metres wide, fills the site's entire street frontage. This sliver of a dwelling packs surprisingly expansive living spaces into a tall and deep volume – harvesting every available inch of inhabitable space out of its highly urban site. Much like Le Corbusier's Beistegui Apartment project – a surrealist rooftop garden penthouse that faced the Arc de Triomphe – this house also performs an act of magic, its kitchen apparently levitating between the city and the sky.

HOUSE IN NIHONBASHI

This extremely thin dwelling packs surprisingly expansive living space into its super-compressive volume.

MEMORIAL HALL IN YAMAGUCHI

The carefully articulated façade addresses its serene garden setting with composed stillness.

MEMORIAL HALL IN YAMAGUCHI

Students, faculty and visitors can relax in the ground-floor lounge, which gracefully opens on to a pond in a garden corner of the campus.

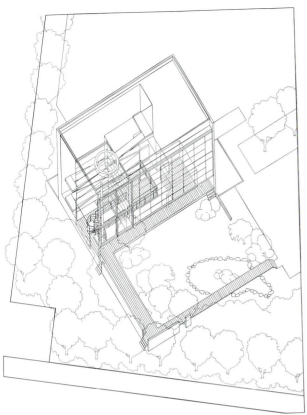

MEMORIAL HALL IN YAMAGUCHI

Axonometric study of the pavilion
building set in a garden alongside
a small body of water.

MEMORIAL HALL IN YAMAGUCHI

A gentle ramp leads visitors to the
multipurpose hall on the third floor.

Waro Kishi has repeatedly acknowledged that his
architecture is neither a form of revivalism nor a denial of
the historical realities that actually make such nostalgic returns
increasingly impossible in today's world. As he has said, '…
certainly, the modern era is already "history" … but despite
this we have not yet entered the next era. We are still living in
the era we understand to be "history". To put it another way, the
modern era is for us both historical and contemporary.' Split
between these realities, Kishi seeks out a temporary suspension
of this paradoxical situation; a gap between now and then; a
logical and valid space for his effective and remarkable creations.

GIN + DESIGN WORKSHOP
SINGAPORE

*Re-engineering
Modern forms
within the speculative
maelstroms of
South-east Asia*

WONG HOUSE

Highly articulated strip windows
recall the work of Schindler
and Wright.

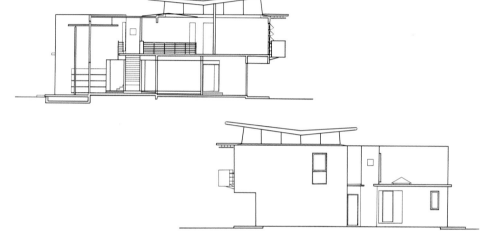

IN SINGAPORE, a city-state that certain European architects
have labelled 'hypermodern' or 'turbo-Metabolist', Ang Gin
Wah is grappling with the meaning of global modernization
in the Asian context. His works attempt to reflect the
assimilation of Asian traditions into the global culture and
the challenge to develop new, specific cultural complexities
for Asia. They are a form of cross-fertilizing experiment
between a traditional Asian architectural idiom and a more
general Modernist language, a positive moment of tension
generating a new and innovative architecture for the
region.

WONG HOUSE

Twin tropical 'butterfly roofs' float
over a fragmented Modernist box
in this major reconstruction of an
existing Singaporean residence.

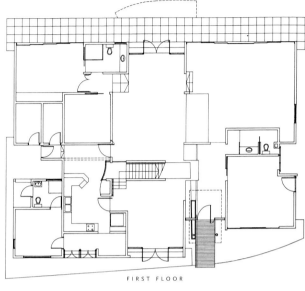

FIRST FLOOR

WONG HOUSE

The animated garden court façade
(ABOVE) glows like a light box at
night. An expressive, cantilevered
balcony (RIGHT) breaks the
symmetry of the rear façade.

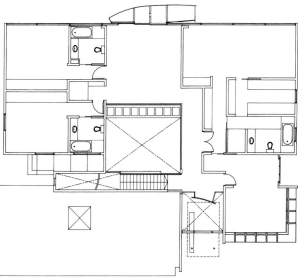

Ang Gin Wah's projects for houses, apartments and cultural facilities in Singapore, Malaysia and Japan focus on what he has termed the 'speculative maelstrom' at work in the contemporary Asian city. As he has written, rapid urban development in Asia has tended to '… smooth out the peculiarities of Asian cultures … so as to accommodate the efficient systems offered by a homogenizing urbanism'. His concern is that the nuances and indigenous cultural landscapes particular to Asia may soon be displaced permanently by the speculative forces at work in its cities, leading to a total eradication of differences. On the other hand, Ang Gin Wah has recognized that overenthusiastic conservation and the careless replication or reproduction of historical types and vernaculars can become a superficial form of resistance to the dynamic

WONG HOUSE

The house's smooth external skin (RIGHT) is complemented by highly articulated clerestory windows.

WONG HOUSE

Living spaces spin off the double-height, top-lit dining room at the centre of the house.

modernization of such cities as Singapore and Kuala Lumpur. Rather than flinch in the face of these realities, Ang Gin Wah seeks to confront increasing Asian modernization on its own terms.

The Wong House, a major reconstruction of an existing residence, is a fragmentation of two floating butterfly roofs and a Modernist pavilion that easily opens on to a large courtyard. It demonstrates the possibility of blurring the distinctions between inside and outside, European and Asian housing arrangements. Its street façade confidently addresses the existing urban fabric with an angular composition that combines several Schindleresque apertures with a double-height entry, which allows

Ee HOUSE

A smooth reductive external skin plays off the roofline's more expressive curvature (ABOVE). Four semi-detached units (RIGHT) are compacted into the house's porous volume.

Ee HOUSE

A delicate steel staircase spills
over an internal reflecting pool.

the interior to spill out generously on to the street at night.
The Elite Park House, also an alteration of an existing structure,
challenges its context of suburban terrace houses with a more
abstract approach. Distinctions between inside and outside are
displaced by a curving glass wall that structures a journey from
the entrance, past private rooms and out on to two 'flying
balconies'. Within the Ee house, enclosure is expressed through
the manipulation of varying layers of transparency and opacity
that respond to the various activities within the house. Spaces
of light and dark, sheer and robust surfaces and a variety of
mobile screen walls create programmatic variations that
oscillate between private and public use. Ang Gin Wah has
opted to treat the modern urban infection in the South-east
Asian city with a stronger dose of the same virus, a re-engineered
modern architecture that has been augmented, in equal parts,
with a local strain of cultural heritage and an appropriate
response to the local climatic situation. As a traditionalist he
understands the need to pass heritage from generation to
generation through building. But Ang Gin Wah has chosen to
work with an unprecedented flexibility and inventiveness that
has replaced stereotypical depictions of Asian tradition with
an acclimatization of Modernist orthodoxy to a subtropical
environment – a truly new architecture for the region.

C HOUSE

This proposal for a residence
in Kuala Lumpur is perched over
a steep incline.

MATHIAS KLOTZ SANTIAGO, CHILE

Recalling lyrically Modern archetypes through a distinctly poetic Chilean architecture

CASA UGARTE

This tiny weekend house is located about 150 kilometres north of Santiago on a spectacular site.

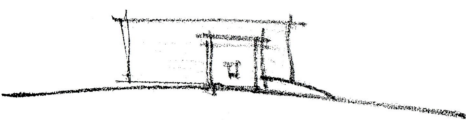

MATHIAS KLOTZ is a young Chilean architect whose prolific output has attracted international respect and already become the subject of a monograph. From his base in Santiago, Klotz has designed and constructed a series of uncomplicated and beautifully composed weekend and vacation houses. His approach is minimal but infused with a poetic richness that sits well in Chile's spectacular landscape. Indeed, it is this tension between the reductive and the expressive that recalls the emblematic and lyrically Modernist archetypes of the Bauhaus and Le Corbusier's purist villas of the mid-1920s.

Casa Müller, one of Klotz's earliest projects, is built against a rugged cliff on a small triangular plateau on Isla Grande de Chiloé, a tiny, isolated South Pacific fragment of land some twelve hundred kilometres south of Santiago. The house is bordered to the south and west by a densely wooded area of arrayanes and to the north and east by the Pacific Ocean.

CASA UGARTE

The house is composed of two wood volumes – one a horizontally clad wedge shape and the other a vertically clad rectangular box – separated by a thin, glazed circulation space.

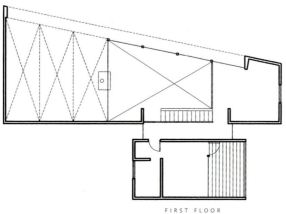

FIRST FLOOR

SECOND FLOOR

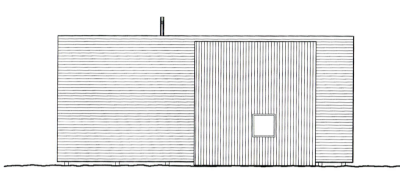

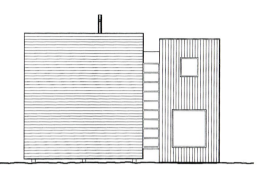

CASA UGARTE

The living area is a light-filled
double-height volume that opens on
to a covered outdoor terrace.

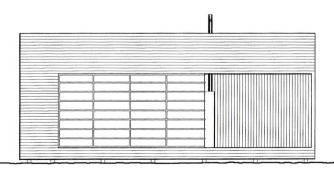

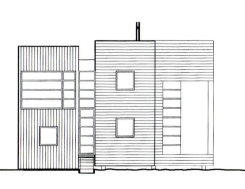

ELEVATIONS

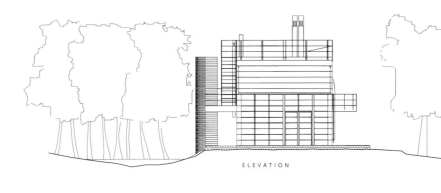

ELEVATION

CASA MÜLLER

One of Klotz's earliest projects,
Casa Müller is built against a cliff
on a small triangular plateau on Isla
Grande de Chiloé – a tiny, isolated
South Pacific fragment of land some
1200 kilometres south of Santiago.
The house is a parallelepiped
measuring seven metres in height
and width and twenty-five metres
in length. At night (BELOW) its
narrow windows emit a warm
glow in a lonely landscape.

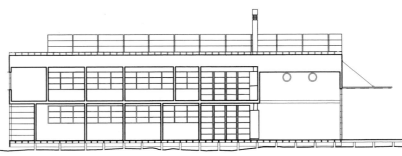

CROSS SECTION

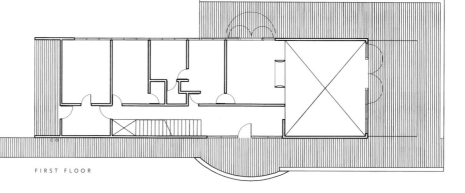

FIRST FLOOR

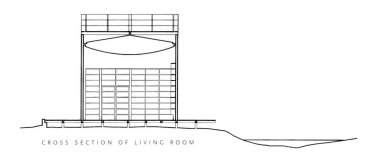

CROSS SECTION OF LIVING ROOM

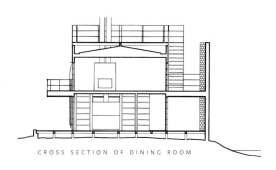

CROSS SECTION OF DINING ROOM

Long and narrow, the house is a parallelepiped measuring seven metres in height and width and twenty-five metres in length. A deepset grid of pillars raises the house forty centimetres over the groundline. A curved wall in cacagua stone shelters and identifies the entrance. Vertically faced in larch planking, the house has narrow horizontal strip-windows, also framed in larch. Railings and stairs are of galvanized steel and the chimneys are finished in copper. Casa Ugarte is a tiny weekend house in Manticillo Sur, about 150 kilometres north of Santiago. Klotz conceived of this house as two wood volumes – one wedge-shaped and horizontally clad and the other rectangular and vertically clad – separated by a thin, glazed circulation space. The smaller volume contains the house's private functions – bathrooms and bedrooms – while the bigger volume holds the public spaces – the kitchen, dining room and study. Covered outdoor terraces provide shelter from the region's fierce south winds. Casa Klotz is further north still, in the region of Playa Grande de Tongoy, a beach area four hundred kilometres north of Santiago. Isolated on a strip of coastline some twenty-four kilometres long, the house is an exercise in reductive geometry and tight planning. Measuring 6 x 6 x 12 metres, the little house is lifted on piers some thirty centimetres over the ground. Klotz faced the house with bleached horizontal strips

CASA MÜLLER

The house's narrow horizontal strip-windows are framed in larch wood.

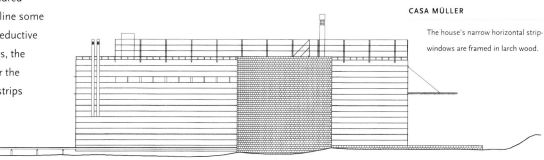

ELEVATION

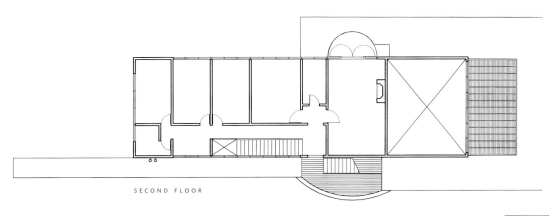

SECOND FLOOR

CASA KLOTZ

Casa Klotz is located in the region of Playa Grande de Tongoy, a beach area four hundred kilometres north of Santiago.

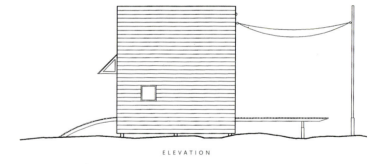

ELEVATION

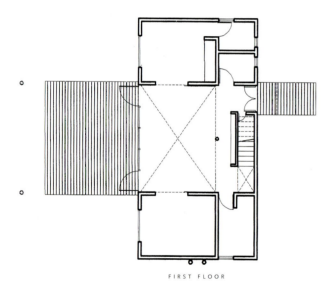

FIRST FLOOR

CASA KLOTZ

Measuring 6 x 6 x 12 metres, the little house is lifted on piers thirty centimetres above the ground.

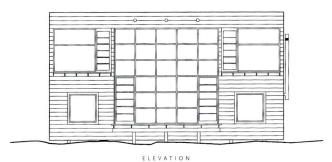

ELEVATION

CASA KLOTZ

A carefully composed glazed 'face'
that allows the double-height living
area to open on to the ocean.

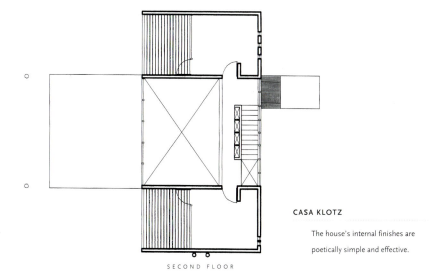

CASA KLOTZ

The house's internal finishes are
poetically simple and effective.

SECOND FLOOR

of wood and a carefully composed glazed 'face', which allows
the double-height living area to open on to the ocean. The
internal parti is poetically simple and effective, while externally
the house's restrained and abstracted volume contrasts with the
vast spaces of its surroundings. Like small boats washed up
on Chile's coast, Mathias Klotz's small and medium-sized
houses are both mysteriously poetic and yet utilitarian objects,
cast into a sublime, remote landscape. His work investigates
the enigmatic Modernist penchant for lyrical form and functional
structure and weaves into this tradition a particular and distinct
Chilean poetry. These simple timber structures can be
understood as nautical hymns that resonate far beyond the
shores of his country.

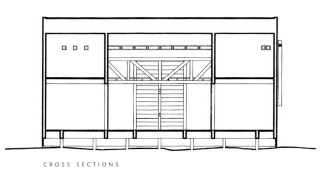

CROSS SECTIONS

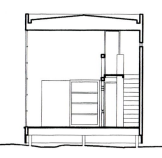

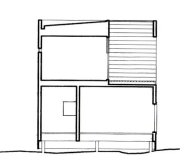

MIKAN
TOKYO, JAPAN

*Knitting a comfortable fit
between urban realities
and Utopian invention*

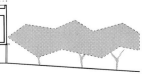

KIRISHIMA ART HALL

The Kirishima Art Hall snakes
through its rural setting on Kyushu.

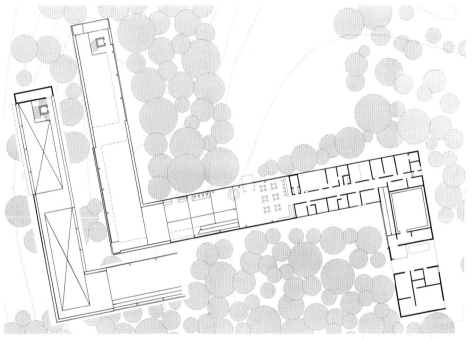

SITE PLAN

KIRISHIMA ART HALL

Mikan's competition entry for a
regional art museum set into a rural
landscape on the southern side of
the island of Kyushu organizes
required exhibition spaces into a
twisted geometrical oblong.

MIKAN IS a vigorous architectural collective composed of four
independent studios, which frequently pool their resources
to undertake large commissions. Although they maintain their
autonomy, these four offices – Célavi Associates, Yosuke
Kumakura Architect, Sogabe Atelier and Atelier Takeuchi –
share more than a studio. Whether working collaboratively or
individually, this 'elastic' Japanese group produces designs for
houses and cultural institutions that both revitalize and challenge
Modernist orthodoxies about space, structure, intent and order.
To them, unlike to their Modernist forbears, absolutes seem
uncertain propositions and what they seek is a comfortable fit
between reality and invention.

The Kirishima Art Hall by Mikan was an entry in a
competition for a regional art museum, to be set in a rural
landscape on the island of Kyushu. The project called for
exhibition spaces, a restaurant, an outer exhibition park and
related facilities. Mikan's design organizes these requirements
into an 'invisible' and instrumental twisted geometrical oblong.
The building's angular shape allows for minimal cutting of the
existing forest and the project is sited along a constant contour
line, effectively burying itself among the trees and blending into
the landscape. The austerity of the volume is counterbalanced
by variations in internal heights and lateral viewlines.

The Kugayama Annex by Atelier Takeuchi is an addition to an
existing house in Tokyo, owned by a young couple. The annex,
shaped by its site and the needs of the client, is wedged between
two existing buildings in order to house their books and a mask
collection as well as to act as a home office. Each of the two lateral
walls is a display area, one devoted to the books, the other to the

CROSS SECTION

The annex is wedged between two existing buildings in a dense part of Tokyo in order to accommodate books and a mask collection.

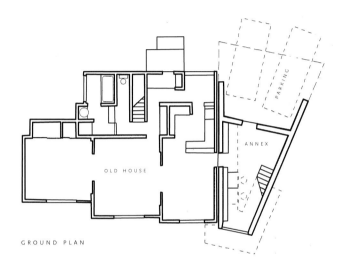

GROUND PLAN

masks. The ends of the wedge provide access and natural light, the rear cantilevering almost three metres in order to allow for two parking spaces.

The NHK Broadcasting Station in Nagano by Mikan is a permanent television station to be used initially for coverage of the 1998 Winter Olympic Games in Nagano. The long, angular volume contains television studios and related facilities. Various formal ideas direct the scheme and group its functions. The chief spatial concept collects the primary components of the station – the studios, their facilities and the technical rooms, administration offices and the entry hall – into what the architects have termed a 'functional iceberg'. External public spaces are woven around this 'iceberg' – in a ground-level courtyard behind a screen of pilotis and on a rooftop garden that affords a panoramic view of the surrounding mountain scenery. The building's public front is covered in delicate aluminium louvres and capped by a tower, which is both a structural device, to support antennae, and an urban sign that displays the multilayeredness of the building.

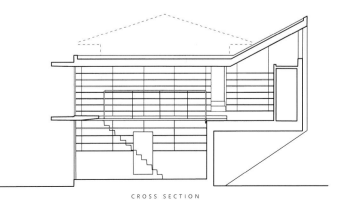

CROSS SECTION

Mikan have stated that they approach architecture without any clear strategy, nor any clear image or definition of what architecture might be. Instead, they try to keep their eyes 'fresh', like those of a beginner. For Mikan, inheritors of the Modernist legacy, restraint is deeply opposed to minimalism, which is the other face of the sublime. Mikan know that 'less is bore', but quite often simple is ideal.

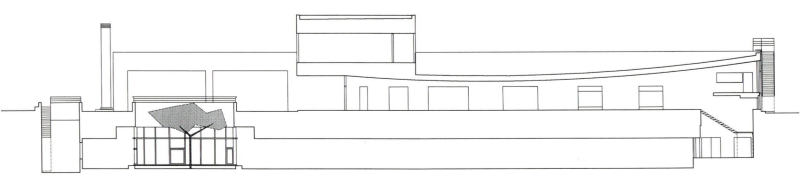

CROSS SECTION

(OPPOSITE) Internal circulation
spaces and an external ground-level
courtyard are woven into and
around the building's regulating
volume.

NAGANO HNK
BROADCASTING STATION

(RIGHT) The NHK Broadcasting
Station in Nagano by Mikan is a
permanent television station to
be used initially for coverage of
the 1998 Winter Olympic Games
in Nagano. The long, slim, angular
volume contains television studios
and related facilities on a site
located some 185 kilometres west
of Tokyo.

TAX (TALLER ARQUITECTURA X)
MEXICO CITY, MEXICO

*Building a confident
Mexican Modernism
within the
contemporary Mexican
cultural landscape*

ADOLF BUILDING

Radial concrete arms support the
structure's cantilevering form.
(OPPOSITE) The building adapts
Modernism to its context.

DANIEL ALVAREZ and Alberto Kalach, principals of Taller Arquitectura X, a youthful Mexico City design studio, represent a new generation of Mexican architects who assuredly merge an urban, Modernist vocabulary with a respect for traditional vernacular forms and an interest in the possibilities of working closely with the Mexican landscape. The Adolf Building, a tall, thin, nine-apartment complex typifies the sorts of well-conceived and simple solutions that TAX develop in response to Mexico City's complex building patterns. According to the architects, this apartment building proposes a new dialogue between an existing building with 'blind', high, vertical walls and the immediate context – a neighbourhood of low to medium-height residential buildings. The design for a house in the Valle de Bravo is an ingenious construction that floats in its setting – a phosphorescent green garden on the slopes of the valley. Enclosed by long brick walls and embedded in the sloping land, the house has four platforms and a pool, which look out over the lush valley. TAX employed a palette of light woods, steel, brick and concrete that blend into a garden of jasmine, aromatic lemon, madereselva, acacia and jacaranda. The recently finished Negro House in Mexico City was realized by the architects as four separate structures floating in a landscape of dense oaks and tepozanes. Set on pre-existing trails so as not to disturb the environment, the house represents a clear and direct organization of concrete, glass, steel and wood. These materials are simply married to achieve an organic unity of space that recalls the works of Frank Lloyd Wright and Rudolf Schindler. Easily TAX's most daring project, the Maguen David Community Center is planned for Cuajimalpa in the state of Mexico. The site for this large religious centre borders a magnificent ravine dramatized by the crater of an abandoned mine. TAX visualize the project as a sculptured citadel at the edge of the cliff face itself. Topography determines each concept for the complex.

The house is a marvellously ingenious construction that floats in its setting – a phosphorescent green garden on the slopes of the valley. Enclosed by long brick walls and embedded in the sloping land, the house has four platforms and a pool, which look out over the lush valley below.

Internal finishes are clearly and directly organized into simple compositions of concrete, glass, steel and wood.

Elements are positioned in relation to the topography while retaining their distinctive representations of the community and its beliefs. The synagogue is the physical and spiritual centre of the complex, a powerful presence in the landscape. Recalling Kahn's dream for Jerusalem – a circle and sphere inscribed concentrically – the synagogue is set like a jewel into the ravine. Light descends into the structure from a great oculus focused on the central area of ceremony. The central synagogue is connected to the Midrash-Seuda Salon and the Great Celebrations Hall by a hypostyle hall of slim steel columns that support a broad plate of water that seems to float among

HOUSE IN VALLE DE BRAVO

An exterior palette of light woods, steel, brick and concrete blends the house into a garden of jasmine, aromatic lemon, madereselvas, acacias and jacaranda.

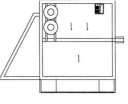

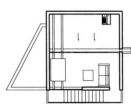

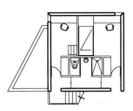

NEGRO HOUSE

Reflecting pools (ABOVE) capture
the house in its magnificent setting.
Inside and outside (LEFT) are
married to achieve an organic
unity of space.

NEGRO HOUSE

Set on a south-facing slope of land
populated with oaks and tepozanes,
this house merges delicately into
the landscape.

GROUND PLAN

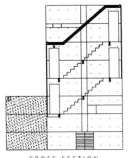

CROSS SECTION

outdoor gardens. This complex is shut off from the street by ridges of vegetation and a citrus grove growing over a parking structure, which is flanked on the north by an administration and services building and on the south by an auditorium and a school. In the bottom of the mine crater a catchment area for water reflects the sky and a library tower rises towards the heavens. Working with the legacy of Louis Kahn's genius and the rich traditions of the Mexican master Luis Barragán, TAX combine elements of both to produce a convincing and powerful architecture.

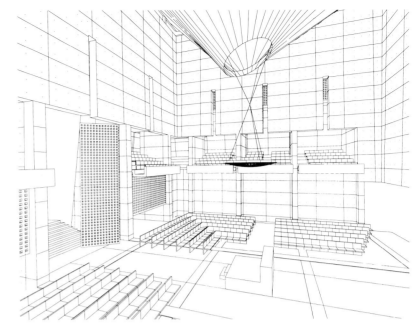

MAGUEN DAVID
COMMUNITY CENTER

Light descends into the structure from a great oculus focused on the central area of ceremony (ABOVE).

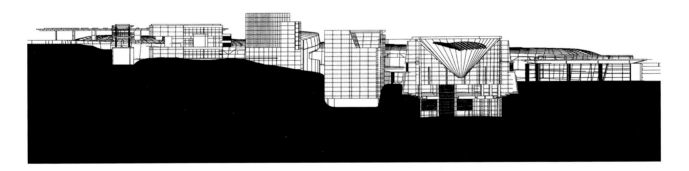

MAGUEN DAVID
COMMUNITY CENTER

TAX visualize the project as a sculptured citadel at the edge of the cliff face itself. Elements of the synagogue are positioned in relation to the complex topography while retaining their distinctive representations of the community and its beliefs.

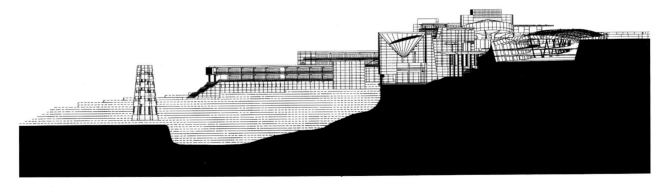

STEPHEN VARADY
SYDNEY, AUSTRALIA

*Retracing the
Modernist fascination
with kinetic form
and unfolding space*

MEASDAY RESIDENCE

This residence involved the
renovation of an inner-city
Sydney terrace house.

MEASDAY RESIDENCE

The building's northern face has
been designed as a layered surface
composed of windows, screens
and sliding louvres that glide
along a track fixed to the external
wall surface.

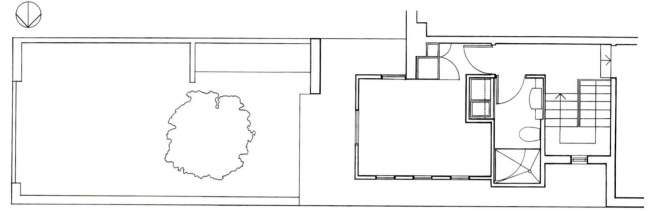

FIRST FLOOR

AUSTRALIAN ARCHITECT Stephen Varady is fascinated by the science
of kinetics and by the work of the avant-garde Russian artist
Kasimir Malevich. His own projects sustain and extend a long
tradition of Modernist works and at the same time reflect these
interests.

The Perraton Apartment project involved the total
reconfiguration of a cramped flat near Sydney's centre. Varady
gutted the apartment in order to insert a brand-new spatial
composition into the shell of the 1960s structure. The new interior
was conceived as a series of intersecting, sometimes movable,
white, rectangular prisms. These pure surface volumes were
inspired by architektons, white plaster architectural sculptures
created by Malevich. Varady closely explored the functional
possibilities of such forms by tying them to specific functional
needs and programmes. To save space, sections of non-load-
bearing walls were removed and replaced with large sliding
partitions. The kitchen was collapsed inside a compact expanding
casement wall, from which various elements, hidden when not in
use, step out, fold down or slide out to allow for food preparation.
Other ideas for saving space include a cantilevered,
counterweighted dining table that folds away to become a wall
mirror and a sculptural television cabinet suspended from a

MEASDAY RESIDENCE

The dining area opens on to a courtyard, allowing for an easy and relaxed mixing of outdoor and indoor space.

MEASDAY RESIDENCE

Varady opened a gap between the addition and the adjoining residence to allow light into the kitchen and living areas.

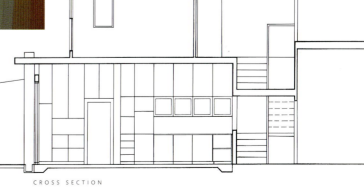

CROSS SECTION

sliding track. The track conceals power and antenna cables and allows for 360° movement and viewing from the kitchen, dining or bedroom areas. Walls are painted white to focus attention on the apartment's views of Sydney's parks and harbour. Carefully placed mirrors capture those views and the reflections in them illusionistically enlarge the small apartment. Finally, the variable nature of the various spatial elements allows the apartment's size, proportion and mood to be reconfigured by the owner to suit different functions and moods.

The Measday Residence, Varady's renovation of a Woollahra terrace house, extended his interest in a kinetic and prismatic architecture. In order to accommodate a variety of functions Varady returned once again to the deployment of a series of intersecting, orthogonal elements within the terrace. Many of these elements recall the early Modern fascination with unadorned planar surfaces and kinetic structures. Varady redesigned the building's northern wall into a layered surface composed of windows, screens and sliding louvres that glide along a track fixed to the external wall surface. These sliding screens and louvres can be adjusted according to the occupants' need for light, privacy or ventilation. The eastern wall is a glass filter that opens on to a courtyard and allows for the easy mixing of outdoor and indoor space. Although often small, Stephen Varady's projects explore big ideas – the long kinetic tradition in modern art that was developed in the works of Duchamp, Moholy-Nagy and Calder, as well as in Malevich's prismatic compositional strategies. One senses in these modest projects a yearning to test these ideas about form and movement on a larger scale and this surely will be the next stage in Varady's development.

PERRATON APARTMENT

The Perraton Apartment project involved the reconfiguration of a cramped flat near Sydney's centre. Varady totally gutted it to insert a brand-new spatial composition into the shell of the 1960s structure.

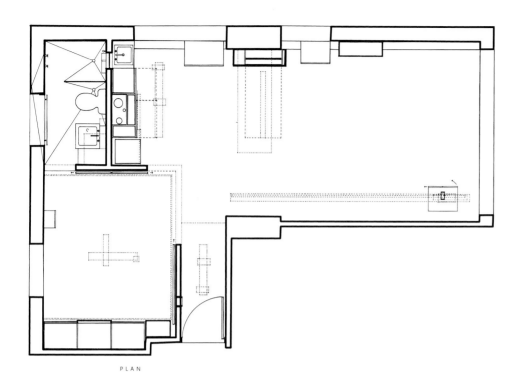

PLAN

Carefully placed mirrors capture
Sydney city views and the reflections
in them seem to enlarge the
small apartment.

PERRATON APARTMENT

The new interior is conceived of as
a series of intersecting, sometimes
movable, white rectangular prisms.

SECOND FLOOR

SLOBAM/PARHAM RESIDENCE

The Slobam/Parham Residence is an alteration and addition to an existing 1960s warehouse in Melbourne, which combines commercial and living uses into a single volume. Sliding irregular sculptural surfaces and a dynamic staircase (RIGHT) animate the house's interior.

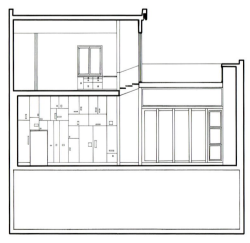

CROSS SECTION

COLLAGE CITIES:
HOMES BEYOND THE RANGE
AARON BETSKY

The cities of the western Americas are urban collages. Drive down the boulevards of Los Angeles or the Reforma and you will find yourself confronting signs in every possible language and in every shape and colour, gesturing through a landscape of glass, steel, concrete and stucco. Despite this cacophony, you still get a sense that these varied appearances have a clear relationship to each other, and not to anything in the land or the air. Together, these structures of the west American city create collages of continuous grids and images, often at a vast scale, floating over a landscape that is not so much mined or used for agriculture, transport or manufacture as it is subjugated to the ultimate logic of urbanization itself.

This collage is only the image of the particular urbanism that characterizes the cities west of the spine of mountains running from the Canadian Rockies to the Andes. The American West is the site of sprawl. It is the place where millions are moving to vast conurbations because that is where there are jobs, housing and entertainment, though not necessarily the kind of infrastructure that might tie all of these together. The tide of construction is thin in the West. It is a layer of expediency laid down by the fast flows of capital as they scoot up, down and around the Pacific Coast. It is up to architects to capture those flows, to anchor sprawl and to make sense out of the collage of continually changing appearances.

These conditions are by no means unique to the western Americas. Everywhere in the world, the traditional notion of the city is giving way to sprawl. Everywhere the collage of signs conquers the static form. Everywhere the construction of a carpet of technology over a landscape scraped down to its most abstract form spreads out into the distance. Everywhere structures last only as long as they throw off a profit, and then disappear into the accretions of disused urban fabric until a new structure replaces them. We live in cities that have less and less of a traditional sense of centre or periphery, but whose order of construction is also more and more defined by the logic of value engineering rather than that of either locally available building materials and patterns of use or of imported notions of style or type. What then makes the western Americas different? It is a question of degree. In North America, the land has not been the subject of permanent, fixed settlement for more than one to two centuries, and often large cities such as Las Vegas or the resort towns of Mexico have grown up in a much shorter time. It is home to the most polyglot population in the

Drive down Pico Boulevard in Los Angeles momentary compositions confront

or the Insurgente
confusion of the
but its immense promise
To see the

history of mankind. Much of it is populated because of its image and its climate, more than because of its natural resources or industry. It is, from the perspective of urban culture, a young place with few roots. In South America, the incredible growth in the population of cities has coincided with the emergence of a global consumer culture that is very quickly wiping out all traces of an indigenous culture with a clear relation in time and space to its particular places.

This does not mean that such places are formless. Look closely and you can find specific physical characteristics in the built environments of the western American cities. First, as noted above, they give the impression of being a collage. Instead of building up forms out of an architecture of walls, they present us with a collection of images and structures. Nowhere is this more evident than in Mexico City, where the concrete or steel grids of many buildings do not hide behind stucco or stone façades, but rather express themselves as open scaffolding supporting skins as varied as Joseph's robe. Glass and signs give the whole a sense of transparency, but also of unreality. The underlying logic of construction is as abstract as industrial techniques have been able to make it over the last few hundred years. The appearance of the buildings comes out of a combination of advertising and Modernism, both of which foreground the consumable visual image as a conveyor of messages (though not necessarily of meaning) in an efficient and sleek manner.

A collage is a collection of pieces. The hybrid nature of these constructions expresses itself as a gathering together of disparate pieces – different materials, with different textures and colours. A collage is also a condensation of many different parts, each of which is present only as a fragment of a larger composition. The buildings of a city such as Mexico City complete themselves in the adjacent constructions or imply forms that could never actually be built. A collage is a form of abstraction, and these buildings perform a purified dance of the basic elements of a technological society. A collage, finally, is a miniaturized mirror of all that is around it. It makes the immense confusion of the urban environment present in the simplicity of a building façade.

The ephemeral quality of these constructions is also evident. They are made out of cheap materials, put together as expediently as possible, and last only as long

In Mexico City, and a parade of modern world, as well. ou with not only the ichness of this tapestry of colours, textures and messages unfold is to realize the sheer energy of this environment.

as any given use. Though these might seem like negative qualities, this lightness also gives the buildings of the American West a delicacy, effervescence and contingency that contrast favourably with the heavier buildings of the cities in the American East. The very qualities that mitigate against monumentality in the western city make it more open, more inviting and more connected to the continually changing culture that permeates it. Instead of monuments, the West has shopping malls, but it also has spaces that flow through open colonnades, interiors that include the landscape outside and images that engage and complete the life of the street up the face of a building.

This latter quality also gives the basic form to many of the buildings of the West. In their character as scaffolding, they become part of the world of consumer culture. They become bearers of advertising, to be sure, but they also partake in the energy of the world around them. The anti-monumentality of the Western city means that buildings can become the formalization and clarification of the urban life, rather than imposing an outside order on them. Because of the climate – but also because of the disconnection this culture has from the land – they are open at their base and in their profile. Instead of presenting a sacred realm separated from the private realm, they can present a rationalization of that world.

The negative interpretation of such an open, collage architecture is that it hides within it the many structures of paranoia. Security systems, air conditioning, plumbing, telephone lines and lighting serve to separate the realm of the building from the landscape around it. Invisible shields, force fields and zones of exclusion define a highly refined environment, a place of 'stims' (stimulation) that feeds off, sucks dry and destroys the vital 'dross' (banality) of the urban environment.

In an architectural sense, it is difficult at first to find any sense of order in this environment. It does not make much sense to look for classical systems of proportion, nor do the clean white lines of a Modernist doctrine appear to be able to give form to the complexities of this world. It is, in fact, not easy to find anything that resembles 'good' architecture or urbanism in these cities. Sprawl, cheap construction, the domination of signs, the scaffolding of technology that echoes the hidden systems of control: all of these elements together create an environment that most observers experience as ugly. Yet I would argue for the beauty of such places. Drive down Pico

Everywhere the sense that we need to live on the very edge the continent, but also of the possibilities ou leads to spik

Boulevard in Los Angeles or the Insurgentes in Mexico City, and a parade of momentary compositions confronts you with not only the confusion of the modern world, but its immense promise as well. To see the richness of this tapestry of colours, textures and messages unfold is to realize the sheer energy of this environment. To see the disparity between this wealth of architecture and either the landscape it has raped all around it or the poverty of those who must try to live within its multitudinous networks is to come to terms with the terrible beauty of an economic system made flesh. For the last two centuries, architects have been trying to do exactly that. They have been attempting to design critical structures that would articulate the nature of these artifices transforming the American West and its inhabitants and, as such, trying to create structures, which, in elucidating the nature of what they are housing, could offer a form of criticism. This has not been the work of most architects, but it has been the task that those architects whose work is worth looking at with a critical eye have set themselves.

Their strategies are rooted in the flexibility of mass construction. The grid work of wood (stick construction), steel (skeleton) and concrete (poured-in-place columns and slabs) liberates the intervening elements to create free-form compositions adaptable to changing needs of everyday life. The Stick and Shingle styles, for instance, developed on the East Coast of the United States, but it was on the West Coast that they stretched into the expansive forms of the Bungalow style, which adapted the free-form spatial arrangements of Japan to the needs of the American family. Steel skeletons gave architects a chance to hang any façade they wanted from a modular structure, but it was on the West Coast that such clothing reached the exuberant excess one can see in the heavily decorated office buildings of the 1930s. Concrete buildings can give form to any number of configurations, but it is only in the self-help neighbourhoods or *favelas* of Mexico and Latin America that it has become a basic structure into which owners can place any combination of tile, brick, glass or glass block that suits their needs, and then extend the spaces, as in a bungalow, to contain whatever needs may arise after the construction of the original grid.

Architects in the western Americas have also delighted in the fantastic. They have erected ladders into the sky, environments that one cannot imagine inhabiting, and

not only of technology offers us, jagged forms pointing towards deformed spatial configurations, which in the sky, the sea or the mind. complete themselves

places of wonder that extend beyond the known into an abstract and indeterminate place in space and time. The pools of Luis Barragán, the courtyard of the Salk Institute, Watts Towers in Los Angeles and the hedonistic realms of Hearst Castle all fall into the category of attempts at making real the Utopia implied by the Manifest Destiny or Cities of Gold, which continues to draw immigrants to these western littorals. These are spaces that affirm the promise, the energy and the beauty inherent in the western landscape, while acknowledging the technological means by which we occupy that space.

A fascination with this technology forms the third component of any critical architecture in the American West. The West is a big landscape that settlers from the

East have long perceived as empty. Their answer has been to build megastructures, from the freeway system of California to the Hoover Dam to the Military Academy outside Mexico City – and even, some have argued, reaching back to the ritualistic monoliths of Aztecs, Mayans, Olmecs, Toltecs and Incas. In most cases, such

Is the true architecture of the American West not which takes sprawl to its logical the themed extreme by creating an anywhere, anyplace

constructions have traced the contours of the landscape, reinforcing them or abstracting them into the lines of exploitation or control. The manmade mesas of the American West give the sense that they are the burial monuments to the western landscape. Artists concerned with landscape forms, ranging from James Turrell to Robert Irwin, landscape architects such as George Hargreaves, and architects such as Barragán or Thom Mayne, though, have been interested in singing alive the rise and fall of the land beyond the attempts by human beings to tame it.

In the twentieth century, architects tried to give shape to the technology so essential to transforming that landscape. The great Modernists of Latin America and the architects who emigrated to southern California from Germany and Austria refined the basic building materials of the American West into the thinnest cages of glass, steel and wood. Theirs was a celebration of our ability to reduce to its smallest, most elegant form the technology that allows us to live in this landscape. Architecture kept pace with the miniaturization of technology, which brought us the grid of electrical, sewage and telephone lines that forms the true, but hidden structure of the western city, but also built the microchip and the automobile.

Together, these forms created an optimistic Modernism as exuberant as anything in the world. From the Case Study programme of Los Angeles to the National University of Mexico City, architects celebrated the sheer possibility of the city of collages. The proposals for the virtual environments of the electro-sphere, as well as the small explosions of glass and steel that still careen off the foothills of those great western mountains, keep alive this dream of building the modern city as a contingent, always-changing Utopia. Everywhere the sense that we need to live on the very edges, not only of the continent but also of the possibilities our technology offers us, leads to spiky, jagged forms pointing towards deformed spatial configurations, which complete themselves in the sky, the sea or the mind. Pioneered by expressive architects from R. M. Schindler and Frank Gehry to Felix Candela, it still occupies the imagination of many young designers.

The reality that such optimism masks, however, haunts the architecture of the American West. The Case Study houses hid their cantilevers behind walls. The monuments of Latin American Modernism became the killing grounds of countless

environment,
instantaneously
for instant consumption?
Is the American West
itself not just a sign, on a vast scale,
for the emergence of a
society sliding into irreality?

protesters. The very profligate nature of the urbanism these structures celebrated has corroded their delicate forms with smog and soot, or hidden them behind the security bars and earthquake reinforcements that guarantee their continued existence. The work of younger architects seems deliberately unstable, insecure or just more extreme, as if it could keep the dream alive by pushing it to the point where it becomes nothing but fragmented gestures: a combination of what Eric Moss has called the 'punch-a-hole-in-the-sky' and the 'first-you-do-one-thing-and-then-another' strategies.

In reaction, many architects have become fascinated with 'dead tech', the disused fragments of technology that act as a kind of *memento mori* for the whole city. By importing these unusable pieces, they resist the transformation of architecture into just another consumable bit of a culture dominated by advertising and economic engineering. Rusted and useless, these shields of steel or ganglia of the guts of building stand as a mute memory of a future that might not always and forever be able to sprawl through the fertile fields of the West. A related tactic is the creation of ironic celebrations of Modernism in collages that highlight the very illogic of their forms, or of a cyborg architecture that absorbs all the technology of the city into its robot-like forms, leaving the planes that reach into the distance, in Neil Denari's drawings, for instance, as the empty blanks they are increasingly becoming.

Not all this work is, of course, so nihilistic or satiric. Many of the best architects of the western Americas still believe that they should keep collaging together the forms they find around them into the colourful, romantic continuations of a tradition of fragmentary wood or concrete construction. From the Miller/Hull Partnership in Seattle to Fernau & Hartman in Berkeley; from Rob Wellington Quigley in San Diego to Alberto Kalach in Mexico City and Glenda Kapstein or Mathias Klotz in Chile, moments of romance still issue from the drawing boards. In Latin America, the vivid colours of a colonial heritage mirror the painted totem poles of the Pacific North West with their own attempts to give a sense that life, however fragile, continues to explode out of the anonymity of the sprawl. Living the collage is a path of beauty for the privileged few who can afford to tame and frame its forms, and architects will always have a role in creating such romantic respites.

It is interesting to note that it is only in the cities beyond the first mountain ranges that an attempt to combine such approaches into the creation of latterday monuments, whose mute and enigmatic form resists consumerism, but which harbour ephemeral oases in a world of sprawl, has surfaced in the work of architects such as Antoine Predock and Will Bruder. It is these rising cities of the West that perhaps offer a different future from the Utopian or dystopian destiny of the coastal areas. Yet these cities and their architecture remain isolated, appearing like instant ruins at the edges of human habitation.

Both of the strategies based on collage, on the other hand, acknowledge the nature of the western city and seek to respond to it, either by building its death mask or by finding within it the possibility of continued rebirth. Neither answers the ultimate challenge presented by such urbanizations today. Given the increased flexibility of technology and the almost total domination of techniques of consumer seduction, is architecture not destined to disappear into the scaffolding propping up the billboard from behind or the smooth plastic of the handheld control device? Is the true architecture of the American West not the themed environment, which takes sprawl to its logical extreme by creating an anywhere, any place, instantaneously for instant consumption? Is the American West itself not just a sign, on a vast scale, for the emergence of a society sliding into irreality?

When 'the big one' that promises to rend the coasts of the Americas asunder finally hits, will not the landscape reassert itself? When we have sprawled from ocean to mountain and transformed everything in between into the thinnest network of technologies of connection holding up an ephemeral collage, will we not drown in the very seamless sameness of such space? When architecture stops finding ways to slow space down, will we not crash? It is such questions that any architecture that would call itself critical must answer if it wants to rebuild the collage cities of the American West into an alternative, more ecologically conscious and humane destiny.

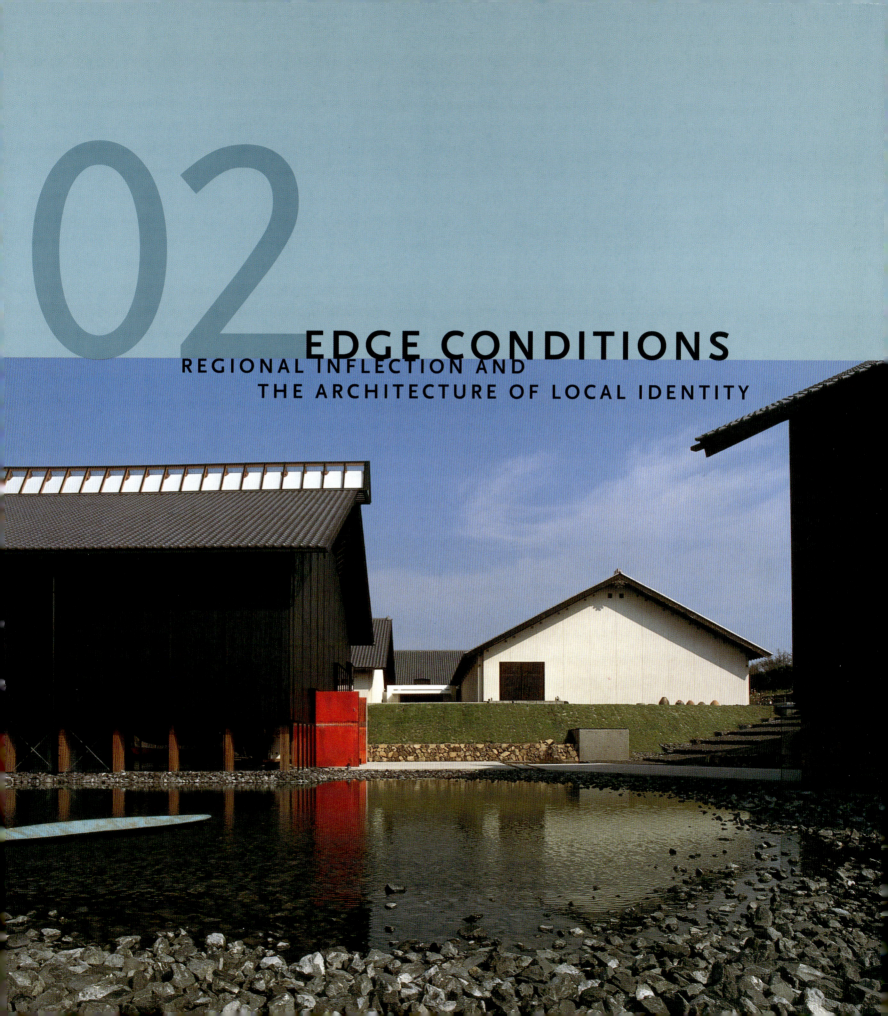

02

EDGE CONDITIONS
REGIONAL INFLECTION AND
THE ARCHITECTURE OF LOCAL IDENTITY

Nowhere in the world are the forces of global modernization, techno-industrialization and the mass media more intense than in the nations of the Asia-Pacific Rim. From the border zones of northern Mexico, where the dominant economic form is the maquiladora, a foreign-owned, locally run manufacturing and assembly plant, to Taiwan, with its busy container port at Chilung, the speed and intensity of trade and culturally driven interchange are astounding. On the West Coast of the United States an average of thirty container ships, each some 230 metres long, depart for Tokyo, China and Singapore every day, carrying over 90,000 tonnes of American goods bound for the East Asian market. In central China, The American Paradise, the first destination golf resort planned for that country, will soon open. This massive complex will include two 300-room hotels, a mountain lodge, vacation villas, a nightclub and an 'American Cultural Village' theme park. No wonder, then, that companies such as Coca-Cola Inc. can claim that, in the 1990s, 'We are not a multinational, we are a multi-local corporation'. No wonder, then, that singular regions, the very individuated cultural zones that define places, peoples and locales have been overridden by what Robert Wilson and Wimal Dissanayake, editors of *Global/Local: Cultural Production and the Transnational Imaginary*, have termed the ever-present flextime of commodity, human, image and information exchange. While this phenomenon has undoubtedly brought jobs, education, wealth and security to many countries that were previously racked by massive poverty, political instability and poor infrastructural organization, in this maelstrom of uncontrollable, geometric development what is often forsaken is the sense of place and history that can distinguish one society from the next. On Planet Hollywood, it matters little whether your ancestors were Aztec warriors or Khmer sculptors – everyone is just another media consumer, a market target. Individuals, once confidently connected to their cultures and landscapes, are cut adrift in a river of never-ending consumer trends, fashion 'innovations' and new-age cult religions. Weak or small cultures are lost in the throbbing, radiant glow of globalized culture, swamped by the incessant flood of transnational media broadcasts and push technologies.

> The term 'Critical Regionalism' is not intended to denote the vernacular ... but rather to identify those recent regional 'schools' whose primary aim has been to reflect and serve the limited constituencies in which they are grounded. Among other factors contributing to the emergence of a regionalism of this order is ... an aspiration at least to some form of cultural, economic and political independence.
>
> Kenneth Frampton, *Modern Architecture: A Critical History*

In response, many cultural producers, especially architects, are returning to the traditional and local customs and habits of their respective regions. Critical Regionalism, as the eminent architectural historian and critic Kenneth Frampton has termed this architecture, offers a vital and increasingly relevant, 'contrapuntal', localized means of spatial production – a self-knowing, hybridized architecture that is informed by both the traditions of place and the benefits of modern technologies.

Regionalist architecture is a relatively recent phenomenon, having developed mostly over the last two decades in the non-Western world. Some of the earliest proponents of a self-consciously regionalist architecture, figures such as Charles Correa and Balkrishna Doshi in India, Rick Leplastrier and Glenn Murcutt in Australia, Mexican Teodoro González de León or Geoffrey Bawa in Sri Lanka, have sought to find poetic ways to reconcile Modernist innovations and tendencies with local needs, climates and traditions. Their successes in creating a line of resistance to the 'optimizing thrust' of universal culture (Frampton's phrase) have been well documented. Their works, notably Bawa's Parliament Building or his own studio in Colombo and Murcutt's delicately placed houses throughout Australia, are careful amalgams of the past and the present; happy resolutions of seemingly incompatible motifs and currents of thought. This is an architecture that considers the past as neither nostalgia nor kitsch but as a source of new ideas and a means of transforming the universalizing Modernist vocabulary into a local idiom that can confidently speak back to the world. Using modern means, these architects and others have dealt attentively with site, local construction techniques and materials, topography and climatic conditions. Such projects undertake to answer the puzzle French philosopher Paul Ricour posed: '… how to become modern and return to sources; how to revive an old, dormant civilization and take part in universal civilization'.

Today, many architects in the Asia-Pacific region are continuing to explore the challenge of blending traditional forms and ideas with modern techniques and concepts. In the Antipodes, Clare Design respond to the landscape, climate and culture with an architecture rigorously developed from both Australian and international traditions. Northern Californian architects Fernau & Hartman successfully extend a specific Bay Area regional tradition begun by the likes of William Wurster. Working in some of Chile's most remote coastal regions, Glenda Kapstein creates works of great consideration that seem to map out a new direction for Chilean architecture while also referencing local materials and mythologies. Legorreta Arquitectos, based in Mexico City, blend pre-colonial, post-colonial and modern elements to create forms that are decidedly Mexican. In Seattle, the Miller/Hull Partnership's explorations and interpretations of modern architecture relate directly to regional influences and climates found in the Pacific North West. Hiroshi Naito's buildings, strongly wedded to historical forms as well as to modern technical solutions, crystallize the conflict between the ancient and the contemporary in Japan today. Through his various projects in and around San Diego, Rob Wellington Quigley argues for the legitimization of the populist vernaculars found in southern California – vernacular architectures that may help define a more meaningful south-western American regionalism.

If there is no going back to a kinder, more gentle past for any of the nations on the Asia-Pacific Rim, then the opportunity to create architectures that reconfigure the historical, cultural and climatic situations specific to a locality, a region or the edge conditions around the Pacific seems not only increasingly relevant for many architects but also a pressing need for the societies within which they work.

FERNAU & HARTMAN ARCHITECTS
BERKELEY, USA

Manifesting vernacular forms and sensitive materiality in the northern Californian landscape

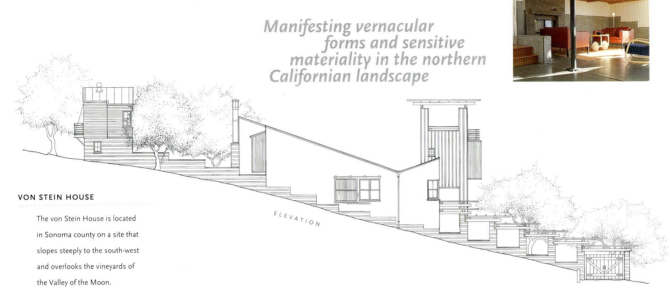

VON STEIN HOUSE

The loftlike bedroom overlooks the living area.

ELEVATION

VON STEIN HOUSE

The von Stein House is located in Sonoma county on a site that slopes steeply to the south-west and overlooks the vineyards of the Valley of the Moon.

AXONOMETRIC STUDY

VON STEIN HOUSE

Two towers punctuate the scheme. The taller, shown here, forms an entry gate through which the primary circulation is threaded. This tower commands the best views of the site, and contains a bedroom/study and an observation/sleeping platform.

FERNAU & HARTMAN'S best-known projects are their deceptively simple, residentially scaled, wood-frame buildings in northern California. These works manifest regional appropriateness and sensitivity to the landscape, together with well-crafted details in combination with a frank expression of materials. In their architectural investigations ordinary buildings are an important source of inspiration. As Richard Fernau states, '... vernacular buildings are sometimes nearly all digression: a collage of

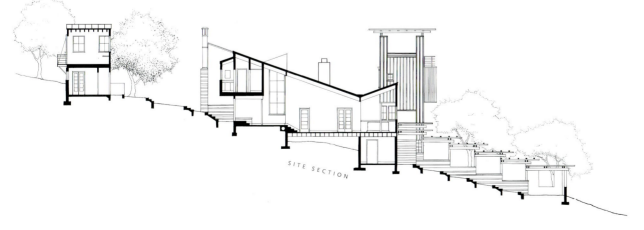

SITE SECTION

adaptive moves performed on more or less generic containers …
what is of interest here is not a set of images but a strategy of
making and the aesthetic that results from it.' The von Stein
House is in Sonoma county on a site that slopes steeply to the
south-west and overlooks the vineyards of the Valley of the Moon.
The project's central organizing device is a wall that crosses the
site, running with the slope, and affords privacy from the road
and adjacent buildings. This wall also serves as a spine that
organizes the project's circulation, structured as a series of
alternating indoor and outdoor rooms that step up the hill.
Two towers punctuate the scheme. The taller tower forms an
entry gate through which primary circulation is threaded. This
tower commands the best views of the site and contains a
bedroom/study and an observation/sleeping platform. The
smaller tower, rising from among the trees in a walled
'philosopher's garden', occupies the corner at the highest
point of the site, where it can benefit from views, privacy and
breezes; this structure serves as a guesthouse.

The Tipping Building is a mixed-use development designed
to accommodate a café, the owner's structural engineering offices
and an urban residence. The building improvises, somewhat
idiosyncratically, on its chaotic urban context – diverse in scale,
activity and style. The hybrid uses of the building are fully
expressed, with the apartment raised and articulated as a unit
rather than obscured in the overall building form. This unit is
itself programmatically articulated with changes of form, material
and orientation to respond to its specific circumstances within
the site. The building's materials – a concrete base, fibre-
reinforced cement panels and wood siding – are drawn, in part,
from the mix of commercial and residential structures near by.

The Cunniff/Fernau Residence was originally a tiny,
undistinguished, flat-roofed, affordable house of the 1950s. The
house was built on the 'carriage house' model, sited on the road
with virtually no setback, leaving a comparatively spacious rear
yard. The primary architectural impulse that guided Fernau &

THE STEVEN TIPPING BUILDING

The building's materials – a
concrete base, fibre-reinforced
cement panels and wood siding –
are drawn, in part, from the mix
of commercial and residential
structures near by.

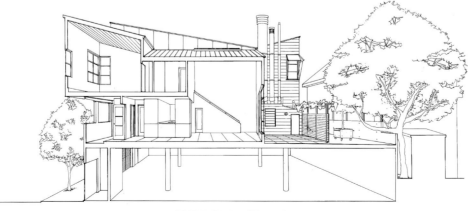

SECTIONAL PERSPECTIVE

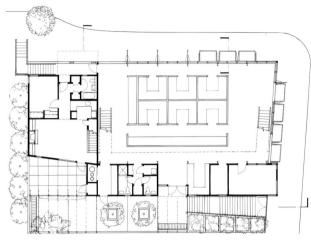

Hartman was to reinforce the urban-rural character of the house by reasserting its 'roadhouse' quality and making a virtue of its location on the street. Throughout the exterior and interior, a range of wood products have been used for their inherent possibilities. This variety includes board and shingle siding, veneered and resin-coated plywoods, fibreboard and exposed framing members. They are combined with various finishes (natural, clear seal, stain and paint) to help differentiate the

THE STEVEN TIPPING BUILDING

The Tipping Building is a mixed-use development designed to accommodate a café, the owner's structural engineering offices and an urban residence.

THE STEVEN TIPPING BUILDING

The hybrid uses of the building are fully expressed, with the apartment raised and articulated as a unit rather than obscured in the overall building form.

CUNNIFF/FERNAU RESIDENCE

The house was originally a tiny, undistinguished house built in the 1950s. Fernau & Hartman built over the older structure but reinforced the urban-rural character of the original house by reasserting its 'roadhouse' quality and making a virtue of its location on the street and relationship to the mature fir, cypress and redwood trees and creek to its rear.

CROSS SECTION

AXONOMETRIC

CUNNIFF/FERNAU RESIDENCE

Access to the sleeping porch is through a movable wall, which slides out from the house and hangs from its track among the trees. The bed itself rolls out on to the sleeping porch, virtually filling it.

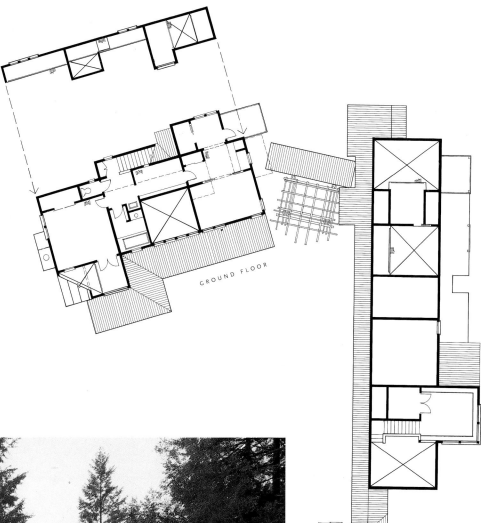

GROUND FLOOR

COLLECTIVE HOUSING FOR THE CHEESECAKE CONSORTIUM

The members of seven households in California, currently moving into retirement, intend to live in this compound. The buildings are designed to respond to the dynamics of group living and 'grow old' with the residents. Low cost and space-saving are important, as are adaptability and capacity for later expansion.

CROSS SECTION

WESTCOTT/LAHAR HOUSE

The Westcott/Lahar House is situated on a gentle, wooded slope that rises above the Bolinas Lagoon in northern California. Designed for a young family as an antidote to an overly compartmentalized urban existence, the house is divided simply into locations for three fundamental activities – eating, playing and resting.

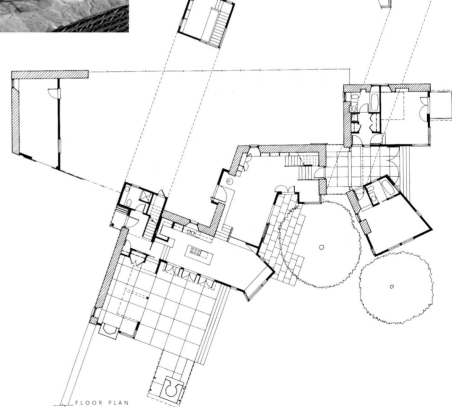

various spaces and interventions. In the north-west corner of the upper level, an underutilized deck was replaced by an enclosed, treehouse-like trellis porch supported on an unpeeled redwood log. A sleeping porch of redwood decking supported by a steel frame is suspended under this space, abutting the redwood log and hanging out over the creek. Access from the master bedroom to the sleeping porch is through a movable wall, which has resin-coated plywood on the interior, redwood siding on the exterior and is framed in steel. This wall slides out from the house and hangs from its track among the trees. The bed itself is mobile and rolls out on to the sleeping porch, virtually filling it.

Fernau & Hartman have refused to adopt a particular style in favour of a way of working that is site- and situation-specific. The architecture that results, while carefully orchestrated at one level, retains an improvizational and circumstantial quality that ties each project to the particulars of its making and to its cultural and regional setting.

FLOOR PLAN

GLENDA KAPSTEIN
ANTOFAGASTA, CHILE

*Creating cities in
miniature against
the infinite landscapes
of Chile's most
remote coastal regions*

RETREAT HOUSE

The lightweight roof above the
children's dining court is framed
in local timbers, which cast a
delicate and mesmerizing shadow-
play over the interior space.

LIKE THOSE in many other Latin American countries, Chile's
relatively young culture is the marriage of a European colonial
heritage, a more remote and ancient indigenous history and
recent American influences, especially in the field of urban
expansion. Chile is a long, slim country, '… a blade, pointed at
the heart of Antarctica', as Henry Kissinger once said. Indeed,
although Chile has over 4,300 kilometres of coastline, the country
is rarely more than 180 kilometres wide at any point. Squeezed for
the most part between the Andes and the Pacific Ocean, Chile is
made up of twelve distinct regions ranging from the desert-like
expanses of the north to the frigid reaches of the far south.
Recognized Chilean architects have usually been based in or
around Santiago. But more recently, some of the most intriguing
architectural projects in Chile have been designed by architects
living well away from the hustle and bustle of Santiago's sprawling
suburbs. Glenda Kapstein is one such architect. Trained at the
University of Chile at Valparaiso, later in Spain and Santiago, and
a long-time collaborator of Ramón Vazques Molezún and José
Antonio Corrales in Madrid, Kapstein works in Antofagasta in
Chile's north. There, she has undertaken several projects while

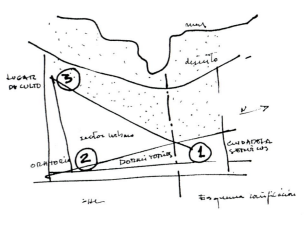

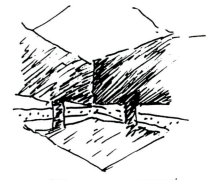

RETREAT HOUSE

Sunken passageways in the
dormitory wing (ABOVE) create
unlimited vanishing points in the
desert landscape. A series of line
drawings (RIGHT) show the robust
relationship of the complex to its
dramatic surroundings.

RETREAT HOUSE

The metal-capped chapel and its forecourt graciously front the expansive sandy plain between the house and the Pacific Ocean.

also teaching in the school of architecture in Antofagasta's Northern Catholic University. Kapstein's Retreat House, or la Casa de Retiro de la Compañía de Jesús, as it is known in Chile, is sited north of Antofagasta, in a district of the city that is bordered by the Pacific Ocean to the west and the Atacama desert to the east. The project is built on a sandy terrain that is occasionally broken by rocky outcrops and terraces. Here, between the desert and the sea, the sky and the land, Kapstein has built a series of pavilions, open corridors and extending promenades that force the inevitable presence of the Pacific Ocean's infinite horizon into sharp focus and provide an appropriate setting for contemplation and solitude. Designed to function like a small city in the desert, the Retreat House is arrayed over the site in several separate sectors that include dormitory blocks, an oratory, gardens, a plaza, small pools, eating units, a chapel and even solar collection facilities.

The architecture Kapstein devised for the Retreat House seems to seek out the silence of the desert and the vast distances of the local landscape. Kapstein suggests that the project has developed as a reading of its setting. Like the local countryside, a space tightly organized by the relations between sand and rock, shifting and permanent landscapes, the Retreat House is ordered into a grouping of fixed monolithic objects set into a series of varying plateaus and basins. In order to accommodate the differing types of sand and rock ground conditions, a system of loose-laid paving slabs was used for the foundations. To prevent slippage, large concrete containers of sand were added to help stabilize the terraces. Walls were built of roughly rendered, reinforced-cement blocks and hollow bricks were laid uniformly to form the floors. Finally, local woods have been applied in batten formations to create parasols and partial enclosures such as the children's dining court. Unlike the more generally late-Modernist approach pursued to the south in Chile's capital, Kapstein's work is distinctly regional, seeking to reference the particular desert-like qualities of Atacama's northern landscape and its distant culture. Her work speaks directly of the infinite horizons found in Chile's north – ponderous spaces that are enframed only by the desert, the sea and the sky.

RETREAT HOUSE

The entrance court orients the visitor's eye to the endless horizon of the Pacific.

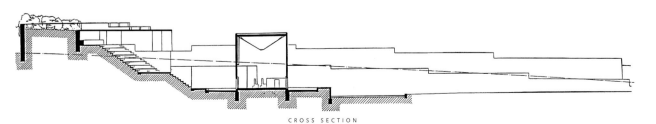

CROSS SECTION

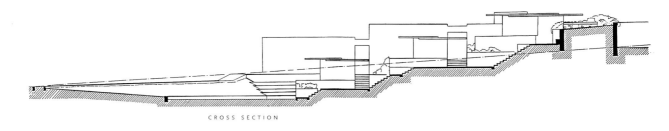

CROSS SECTION

LEGORRETA ARQUITECTOS
MEXICO CITY, MEXICO

SECOND FLOOR

Melding pre-colonial elemental Mexican forms and the Modernist ideal

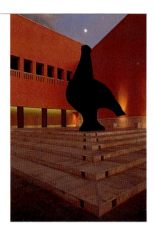

MARCO CONTEMPORARY ART MUSEUM

The courtyard features a sculpture by renowned Mexican sculptor Juan Sorriano.

MARCO CONTEMPORARY ART MUSEUM

The MARCO Contemporary Art Museum in Monterrey, Mexico, was inspired by the traditional plan form of the Mexican house – a deep central courtyard edged by an arcade which allows access to adjacent spaces.

RICARDO LEGORRETA is an imaginative and prolific architect whose buildings, while irrefutably modern in programme and function, are steeped in traditional Mexican spatial forms and means of fabrication. Legorreta has developed a strong framework of ideas and spatial concepts, which builds on his mentor Luis Barragán's poetic adaptations of the Mexican vernacular to Modernist ideals. Like Barragán's, Legorreta's buildings are characterized by their controlled use of viewlines, deep-walled structures, elemental geometric configurations, water features and highly textured polychromatic planar surfaces.

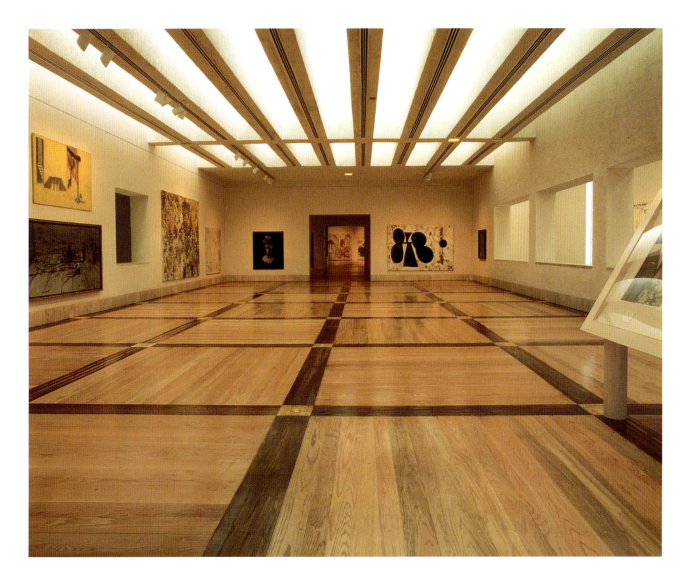

The galleries are varied in height, filled with natural light and flexibly planned to encourage curatorial experimentation. Stern but vibrant exterior walls (BELOW) contrast strongly with the museum's welcoming interior.

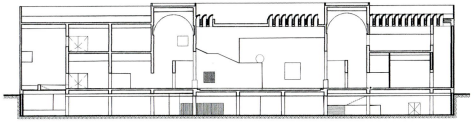

CROSS SECTION

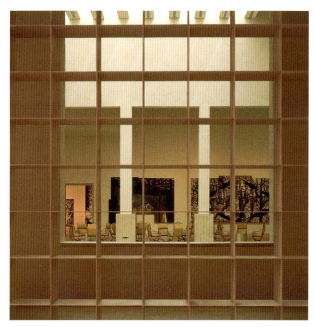

The MARCO Contemporary Art Museum in Monterrey, Mexico, was inspired by the traditional plan form of the Mexican house – a deep central courtyard edged by an arcade which allows access to adjacent spaces. Stern but vibrant exterior walls contrast strongly with the museum's welcoming internal spaces. Access to the museum is through an entry plaza, which features a sculpture by Mexican artist Juan Soriano, a gigantic dove that pays homage to Luis Barragán's pigeon-house. Beyond the entry plaza is the courtyard itself, which gives access to all the

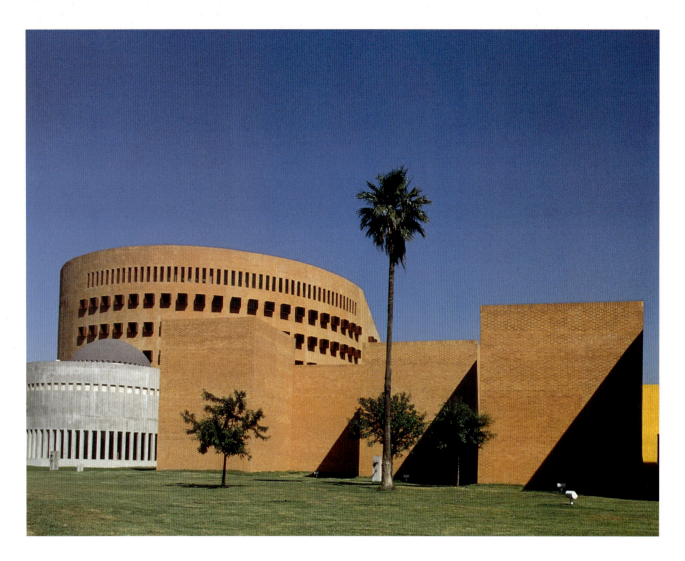

Legorreta's design for the Monterrey Central Library (LEFT and OPPOSITE) was challenged by a difficult site on a lake and next to a park. The library is composed of two basic geometric elements – a cube and a cylinder – embedded in each other. These elements terminate in a diagonally descending point that forks off the library's great rounded body five storeys down into the lake.

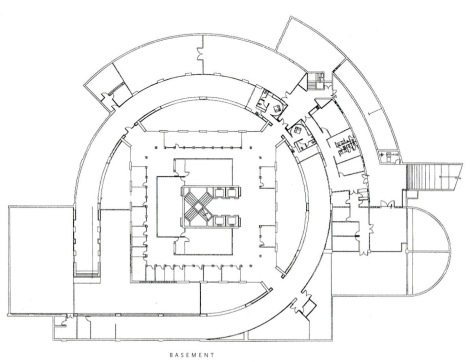

BASEMENT

museum's galleries and also doubles as a space for public concerts, receptions and gatherings. The galleries are varied in height and flexibly planned to encourage curatorial experimentation. In his design for the Monterrey Central Library in San Nicolás de los Garza, Nuevo León, Legorreta had to meet the challenge of a difficult site on a lake and next to a park. Recalling Louis Kahn's monumental compositional strategies, the library is composed of two basic geometric elements – a cube and a cylinder – embedded in each other. These elements terminate in a diagonally descending point that forks off the library's great rounded body five storeys down into the lake. Surfaced mostly in brick, this bold geometric composition creates a public landscape set against the park's greenery and the lake itself. The cube houses 50,000 volumes in four spirally arranged quarters. Reading rooms are inside the cylinder, a fluid space that offers views of the park.

Surprisingly, the Metropolitan Cathedral in Managua, Nicaragua, is Legorreta's only religious building, although his

The cube houses 50,000 volumes
in four spirally arranged quarters.
Reading areas (BELOW) have views
to the park and lake.

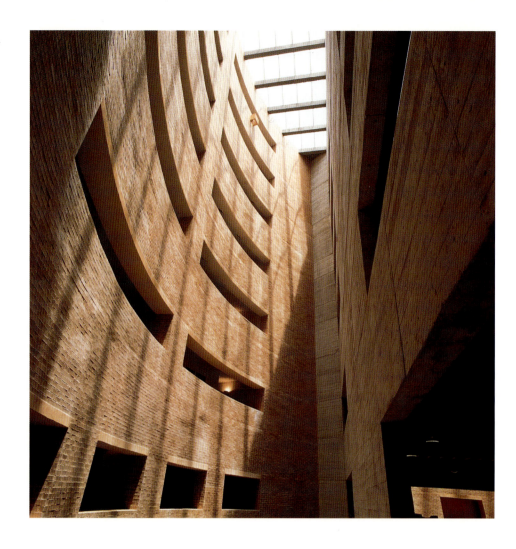

work is often spiritual in nature. The cathedral is a replacement
for an older cathedral, which received extensive, irreparable
damage in the 1972 earthquake that destroyed much of Managua.
In Legorreta's design, sixty-three domes rise over and around a
large, poured-in-place concrete volume. The chapel, bathed in
light delivered by the domes, is a richly hued interior that evokes
the richness, particularity and beauty of Latin American faith.

Ricardo Legorreta's buildings pay tribute to traditional
colonial spaces – the hacienda, the cloister, the mission – but
are also rooted in a pre-Columbian past. Like Barragán, Legorreta
reacts in his works to the sober restraint of an imported
Modernism but without descending into caricaturizations of
nationality and origin. But if Barragán's best works were usually
of a residential nature, Legorreta has confidently 'scaled up' his
spatial syntax to produce public and institutional buildings that
successfully combine pre-colonial Mexican and international
Modern forms.

METROPOLITAN CATHEDRAL, MANAGUA

This project, Legorreta's only religious building to date, is a replacement for an older cathedral, which received extensive, irreparable damage in the 1972 earthquake that destroyed much of Managua.

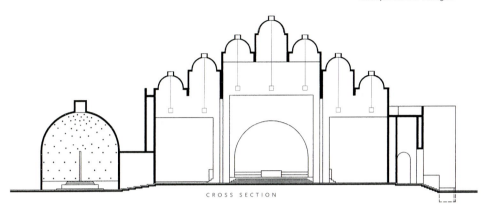

CROSS SECTION

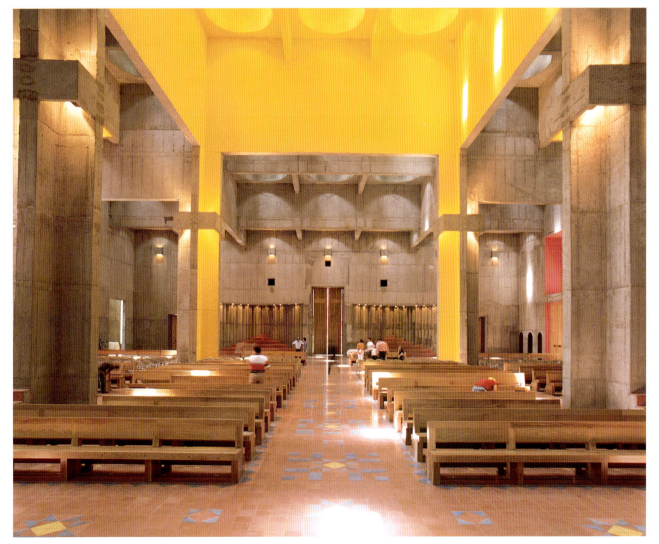

METROPOLITAN CATHEDRAL, MANAGUA

Sixty-three domes rise over and around a large, poured-in-place concrete volume that is earthquake-resistant and chiselled by hand. The chapel, bathed in light delivered by the domes, is a richly hued interior that evokes the richness, particularity and beauty of Latin American faith.

MILLER/HULL PARTNERSHIP
SEATTLE, USA

Pursuing a rigorously logical formal language based on the cultural and building traditions and climatic constraints of the American Pacific North West

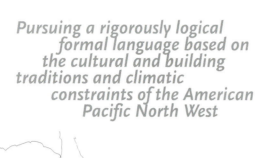

ISLAND CABIN

The Island Cabin (LEFT and OPPOSITE) on Decatur Island in the San Juan Island chain, is a light timber structure perched on a steeply sloping site, which terminates at an abrupt rock cliff over the water's edge.

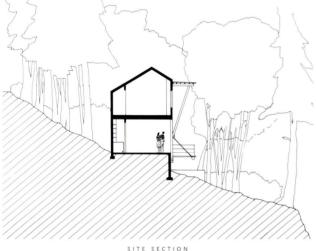

ISLAND CABIN

The upper-floor post-and-beam construction extends out of the solid lower walls and on this level of the house a deep two-metre overhang extends out to protect the outdoor decks.

SITE SECTION

SINCE DAVID Miller and Robert Hull founded their practice in 1977, the firm has pursued a rigorously logical design approach that articulates a formal language closely based on the cultural and building traditions and climatic constraints of the American Pacific North West. The resulting body of work expresses powerful concepts in lyrical forms. Miller/Hull's design philosophy centres around two essential architectural ideas. One is to use a building's structure to create a significant place within a site, and the other is to be sensitive to climate and to respond directly to environmental demands.

The Island Cabin, located on Decatur Island in the San Juan island chain, is a 78-square-metre structure perched on a steeply sloping site, which terminates at an abrupt rock cliff over the water's edge. The cabin is entered over a bridge that leads on to the upper-floor living/kitchen/dining area. The upper-floor post-and-beam construction extends out of the solid lower walls and on this level of the house a deep two-metre overhang extends out to protect the outdoor decks. Exterior elevations are reminiscent of forest-service lookout stations with 'punched' windows. The Marquand retreat in Naches Valley, Washington, faces down into a beautiful river valley rimmed by basalt cliffs. The owner challenged Miller/Hull to construct a limited, two-room programme using materials that were resistant to fire, wind and intrusion. The retreat house's simple geometric form is composed of clearly articulated materials. The architects' stated aim was to produce a building that is truly 'Western' in character without being nostalgic or clichéd. The structure was conceived as a thin metal roof floated across a very basic, concrete rectangular block. The roof provides a shaded porch to the south, clerestory window slots at the main shell and a covered path out to the water-cistern tower to the rear of the building. The 3 x 3-metre opening facing south has two full-size glass and screen sliding doors, which allow the owner to customize the proportion of open ventilation

MARQUAND RETREAT

The retreat house's simple geometric form is composed of clearly articulated materials – a thin metal roof floated across a very basic, concrete rectangular block.

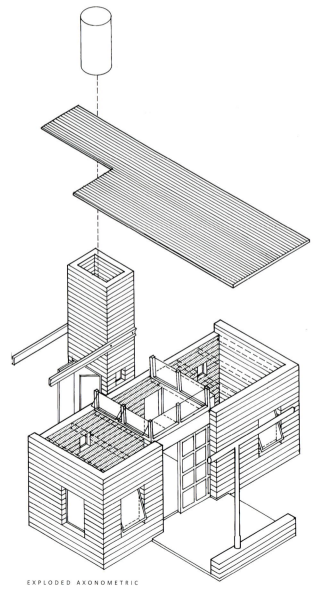

EXPLODED AXONOMETRIC

MARQUAND RETREAT

The Marquand retreat, in Naches Valley, Washington, faces down into a beautiful river valley rimmed by basalt cliffs.

OLYMPIC COLLEGE, SHELTON

The Olympic College satellite campus is a two-phased project. Phase 1, shown here, includes housing, classrooms, administrative spaces and a daycare centre. Environmentally conscious 'green architecture' strategies were used in both site planning and building design. The campus derives its character from the existing naturally wooded setting.

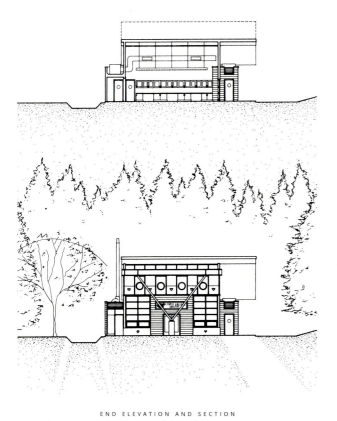

END ELEVATION AND SECTION

to glazed area, thereby responding to the potential for both blistering heat and freezing cold. Without permanent power, the tiny structure is effectively heated by a wood stove. The cistern is currently filled by a water truck; there are plans for a well to be dug in the future. The Olympic College at Shelton deploys environmentally conscious 'green architecture' strategies in both site planning and building design. The result is the beginning of a two-phased campus development that is ecologically sound and derives its character from the existing naturally wooded setting.

The Miller/Hull Partnership's explorations and interpretations of modern architectural design are a response to the extraordinary beauty of the Pacific North West environment. Their projects have an unusually clear fit to their sites and settings.

OLYMPIC COLLEGE, SHELTON

The building's articulated timber structure creates a significant place within its sensitive setting. The interior of the daycare centre (LEFT) is conceived of as a light-filled play area.

HIROSHI NAITO
TOKYO, JAPAN

Addressing the conflict between the ancient and the contemporary in Japan today

CHIHIRO ART MUSEUM

The Chihiro Art Museum in Azumino stands in a quiet rural area with Japanese alps in the background.

CHIHIRO ART MUSEUM

Naito's central idea for the project was to incorporate the building into the existing scenery.

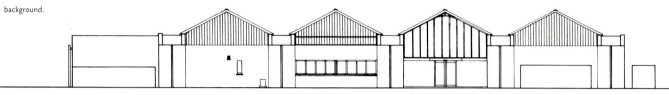

ELEVATION

CHIHIRO ART MUSEUM

An elegant 7.2-metre-span wood roof structure sits on concrete walls and beams. Their slender and elegant profiles provide a wonderful organic internal cadence within the gallery spaces.

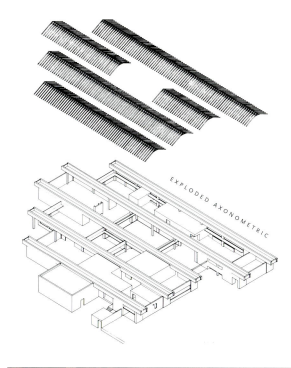

EXPLODED AXONOMETRIC

CHIHIRO ART MUSEUM

Naito applied a rigorous structural logic to the project.

HIROSHI NAITO is an architect whose varied designs for residential and public/institutional buildings are strongly wedded to historical Japanese forms yet employ thoroughly modern technical solutions. His work takes full cognizance of the conflict between the ancient and the contemporary in Japan today.

The Chihiro Art Museum in Azumino stands in a quiet rural area with Japanese alps in the background. It is designed to exhibit the work of Chihiro Iwasaki, an illustrator for picture-books. Naito's central idea for the project was to incorporate the building into the existing scenery. After studying various roof configurations, he decided on a series of consecutive gable roofs

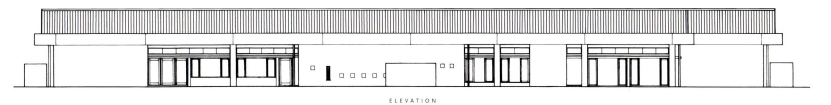

ELEVATION

SHIMA ART MUSEUM

This small museum stands on the
hill next to the Sea Folk Museum in
Mie Prefecture. It was designed to
exhibit oil paintings by
contemporary Japanese artists.

SHIMA ART MUSEUM

Naito created a rich but simple
space defined by pronounced
vertical structural frames, exposed
concrete bearing walls and a simple
roof of laminated wooden beams
and steel tension members.

in order to make the volume of the building look smaller. The
material he chose for the traditional timber construction required
a 7.2-metre-span wooden roof structure, which sits on concrete
walls and beams. A rigid frame was designed at the top of the
gable and the timber rafters were set directly on the top of the
concrete walls that carry lateral loads. These devices enabled the
timber members to be reduced to their slender and elegant
profiles. The Shima Art Museum exhibits oil paintings by
contemporary artists. For this project Naito aimed to create a
rich space by using simple structural configurations and modest
materials. An exposed concrete bearing wall was chosen as the
primary structural system. On top of this, Naito then set a simple
roof constructed of laminated wooden beams and steel tension
members. Finally, a refined glass skylight was inserted in the
sensitive wooden structure that spans the rough concrete walls.
The wooden roof supports traditional Japanese tiles, chosen to
bring visual unity to the site.

The Sea Folk Museum collects, stores and exhibits the
everyday tools of the traditional Japanese fishing industry.
Because of Japan's rapid economic growth during the twentieth
century, many traditional tools have been abandoned in favour
of more modern means and the skills required to use them have
been lost to history. Working within a low budget, Naito chose to
focus the design on the concept of a good, simple shelter.

SEA FOLK MUSEUM

The Sea Folk Museum collects, stores and exhibits the everyday tools of the traditional Japanese fishing industry in a calm setting near an ocean inlet.

SEA FOLK MUSEUM

The Sea Folk Museum is an unobtrusive addition to its unspoilt setting.

HIROSHI NAITO

SEA FOLK MUSEUM

The museum's wood structure
expresses both a Modernist
rationality and the organic
structural forms of Japanese
vernacular buildings.

SEA FOLK MUSEUM

Exhibition areas feature a delicate
laminated-wood roof structure. The
exterior roof surface is finished in
traditional Japanese tile roofing.

He employed traditional materials such as tile roofing and
the combination of old and new technologies to meet the
requirements of cost and durability. Storage areas in the
museum are covered with post-tensioned precast concrete
and exhibition areas feature a delicate, laminated-wood
structure.

As Vittorio Lampugnani has written, to appreciate Naito's
architecture, '… you have to reflect upon the links with tradition
and upon the cultural implications. You may not like some choice,
you may not like some detail. But you will respect the effort and
the consistency of it all, and you will not be able to escape its
powerful presence.'

SEA FOLK MUSEUM

Naito's exquisite design for the
timber roof structure (OPPOSITE)
demonstrates his commitment to
traditional forms of craft and
construction.

ROB WELLINGTON QUIGLEY
SAN DIEGO, USA

Exploring southern California's utilitarian vernacular as a noble and civic architecture

SHERMAN HEIGHTS COMMUNITY CENTER

The courtyard is animated by traditional southern Californian building elements.

SHERMAN HEIGHTS COMMUNITY CENTER

Quigley's scheme for a community centre is located in a multicultural residential neighbourhood close to San Diego's core.

ROB WELLINGTON Quigley is the principal of an eleven-person practice, with offices in San Diego and Palo Alto and whose numerous projects for homes, housing complexes and public buildings convincingly demonstrate that southern California's popular vernacular forms – the light wood frame and stucco beach shack, even the tilt-slab office warehouse – can offer a valid and meaningful foundation for the development of a south-

western American regionalism. Quigley himself has written at length about the Californian populist vernacular, bravely suggesting that, '… in its rare pure state, untouched by architects trained in the art of "good taste" and shaped wholly by market forces, it has a certain perverse charm … In a country that is fast minimizing the differences between cultures and regions, the search for a locally meaningful architecture is more and more relevant.' Quigley's scheme for a community centre in Sherman Heights, an old, vibrant, multicultural, residential neighbourhood close to San Diego's core, consists of a new, 1,160-square-metre building, a restored, two-storey Victorian house and an adjacent pocket-sized park. The project can accommodate lectures, performances, banquets and parties. Traditional southern Californian building elements such as a covered porch and verandah animate this garden court and invite users into the

SHERMAN HEIGHTS COMMUNITY CENTER

The project involved the design of a new 1,160-square-metre building, a restored, two-storey Victorian house and an adjacent pocket-sized park.

SHERMAN HEIGHTS COMMUNITY CENTER

Traditional southern Californian building elements such as a covered porch and verandah animate this garden court and invite users into the centre.

SHAW LOPEZ RIDGE

Shaw Lopez Ridge is a twenty-four-house subdivision located between a large developer-oriented housing project and a rustic canyon preserve.

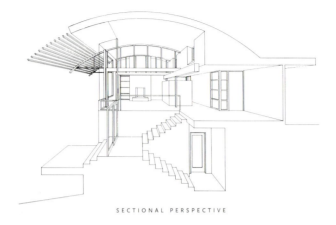

SECTIONAL PERSPECTIVE

SHAW LOPEZ RIDGE

Glazing is biased to the southern sun and view and shaded by curving louvres.

FIRST FLOOR

SHAW LOPEZ RIDGE

Simple and flexible in floor plan,
each two-level house has a
corrugated-metal vaulted roof that
is constructed of concrete block,
wood frame and stucco. Movable
shoji screens and optional
bookcase walls make a variety
of living arrangements possible.

centre. The Solana Beach Transit Station is part of a mixed-use
development project that eventually will include retail and
restaurant space, low-cost housing for senior citizens, artist lofts
and townhouse-style apartments and act as the new town centre
for this growing beach city. Quigley employed design imagery
inspired by the Second World War structures and greenhouse
sheds still found throughout southern California and designed a
park around the station that creates a rural illusion and is inspired
by the nearby sandstone cliffs and beach access stairs. Shaw
Lopez Ridge is a twenty-four-house subdivision located between
a large developer-oriented housing project and a rustic canyon
preserve. The development is given shape and character by the
tight linear 'wall' the houses follow along the uphill side of the
street. Simple and flexible in floor plan, each two-level house has
a corrugated-metal vaulted roof that is constructed of concrete
block, wood frame and stucco. Subsidized by the Housing and
Urban Development authority, 202 ISLAND INN is a low-cost 197-
unit SRO (single-room-occupancy hotel) at the edge of downtown
San Diego's Chinatown district. Each of its three different street
façades responds to particular and immediate urban design

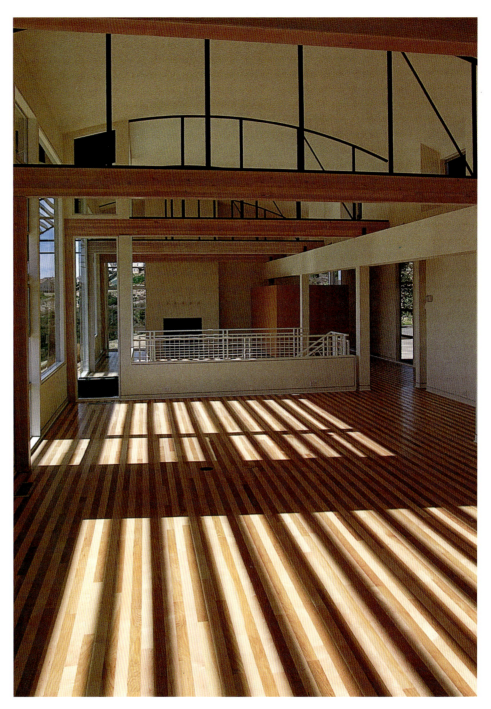

SECOND FLOOR

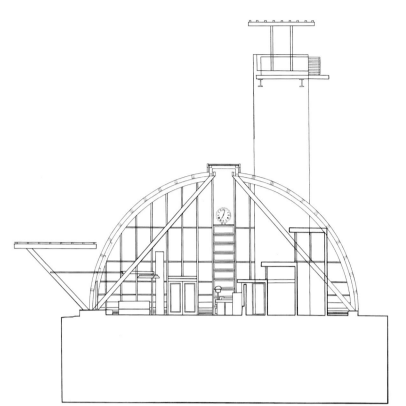

CROSS SECTION

SOLANA BEACH
TRANSIT STATION

The train station acknowledges the vaulted typology of its European origins, but responds more specifically to local traditional forms such as Second World War military structures and greenhouse sheds.

SOLANA BEACH
TRANSIT STATION

The Solana Beach Transit Station is part of a mixed-use development project that will act as the new town centre.

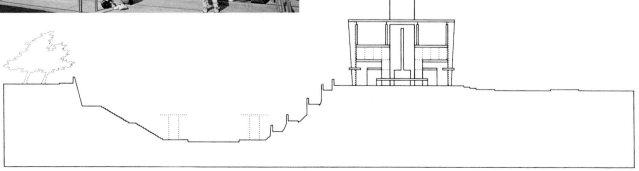

CROSS SECTION

CAPISTRANO BEACH HOUSE

This house is set in a strip of narrow lots between the ocean and a windswept bluff in a small Californian beachfront community.

opportunities. Quigley strongly feels that in southern California the opportunity to create a more authentic built environment may lie in the struggle to weave an architecture of cultural diversity. The '…real Arcadian Dream,' he says, 'will not be a blending, but a colourful, distinct collage of dislocation.' He is interested in a celebration of a local architecture as a form of localism, understood not as an end in itself but as a means of transcending provincialism and enriching his own cultural reality. Rather than subvert the conventional Californian ways of building and detailing, Quigley tries to embrace and co-opt the status quo in order to '… explore the utilitarian vernacular and its intriguing possibilities as a noble and even civic architecture.'

CAPISTRANO BEACH HOUSE

The tall glass walls of the pavilion sweep around the garden and bathe the living area in rich light.

202 ISLAND INN

202 ISLAND INN is a low-cost 197-
unit SRO (single-room-occupancy
hotel) at the edge of downtown San
Diego's Chinatown district.

202 ISLAND INN

Each of its three different street
façades responds to particular
and immediate urban design
opportunities.

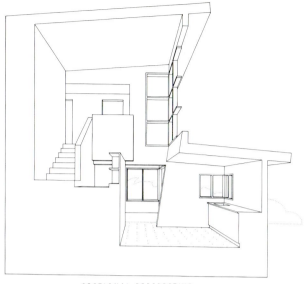

ESPERANZA GARDENS APARTMENTS

The Esperanza Gardens Apartments complex is the first new affordable housing project built in the southern Californian community of Encinitas in over twenty years. It is patterned after the classic bungalow court apartment complexes found throughout southern California.

FIRST FLOOR

SECOND FLOOR

FIRST FLOOR

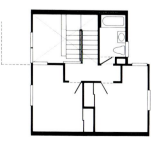

SECOND FLOOR

CLARE DESIGN
SUNSHINE COAST, AUSTRALIA

Responding to the Australian landscape, climate and culture with an architecture developed in part from regional and international traditions

HAMMOND RESIDENCE

The Hammond Residence is sited on a remote hill overlooking the panoramic Sunshine Coast on Australia's north-eastern coastline.

KERRY AND LINDSAY Clare respond to the specific qualities of the Australian landscape, climate and cultural conditions with an architecture that is specifically regional but also tied to certain universal Modernist traditions. They have set out to create a locally responsive architecture capable of expressing the cultural and geographical forces that shape it. Their work focuses on observing traditional Australian construction methods and techniques and reveals how local knowledge, common sense, intuition and dialogue can assist in determining what is relevant to the development of a region. Based in south-east Queensland, the Clares have designed and built more than one hundred projects, most within fifty kilometres of the Pacific Ocean. Michael Keniger has noted that the Clares' many schemes show '… respect for Queensland's traditional timber houses with their lightweight, single-skin construction, shaded cores and verandah-ed fringes …'

The Clares' early interest in Scandinavian architecture, in particular the works of Alvar Aalto, has led them to observe that a regional architecture can be disciplined by landscape and climate and in turn respond to a specific culture with innovation and without sentimental or provincial leanings. The Clares' prime motivation has been to direct this knowledge towards the history, nature and quality of Australian habitation.

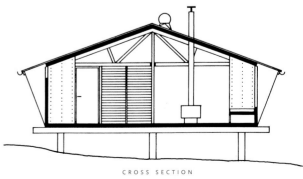

CROSS SECTION

HAMMOND RESIDENCE

Owing to its remote location the house required the use of many prefabricated and precut elements in a unique and innovative way.

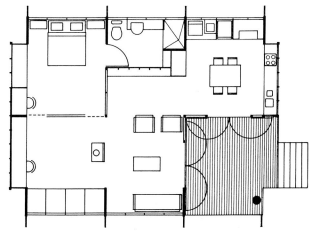

GROUND FLOOR

HAMMOND RESIDENCE

The house draws its constructional logic from the vernacular building tradition in Queensland while also employing contemporary ecological design principles.

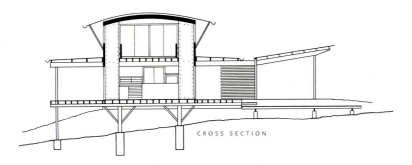

CROSS SECTION

Around the turn of the century, in the northern parts of Australia many people lived on verandahs – outdoor spaces which were originally designed to shade and shelter the external walls of Georgian-inspired dwellings. However, as the verandah became inhabited, it was quickly supplemented with various screening devices that gave expression to the pleasures of outdoor living. This unselfconscious tendency has positively affected the architecture of the region and deeply influenced the Clares' response to their setting. Like other Queensland architects, notably Gabriel Poole and John Mainwaring, the Clares have investigated alternative ways of living. They have successfully combined the Modernist tendency for universally opened space with the historic, locally appropriate, fabulously light and delicate tropical architecture of the region. Their designs for such dwellings as the Hammond House or the Cotton Tree housing project are particularly open in feel and emphasize communal spatial relationships.

As Keniger has noted elsewhere, the Clares' practice is '… characterized by a concern for placemaking in response to the

CLARE RESIDENCE

The residence's ply-framed, multiple-'fin' structure pushes the building's loads to its perimeter envelope, creating a free-plan living space at ground level that can be easily opened to ventilate the interior. The clear and open plan (RIGHT) allows for full-width spaces that take advantage of landscape and ocean views while also allowing natural light to penetrate deep into the house.

FIRST FLOOR

CLARE RESIDENCE

(OPPOSITE) The Clare Residence is a two-storey, colourful, 'timber box' that takes maximum advantage of its site, positioning itself to catch sea breezes, views and sunlight. The corrugated-iron skin is punctured by deeply louvred window recesses and bands of continuous glazing around the top floor.

RAINBOW SHORES

This multi-unit housing project is the first stage of a small town that will be built in a significant coastal location formerly cleared by mining operations.

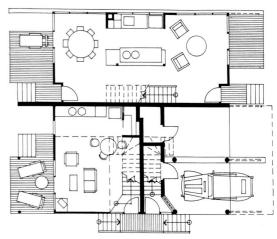

FIRST FLOOR

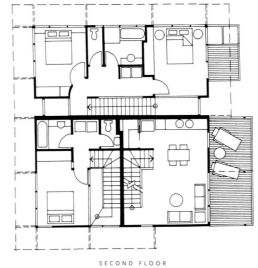

SECOND FLOOR

CROSS SECTION

RAINBOW SHORES

This development achieves a surprising density of approximately fifty dwellings per hectare while respecting existing groves of trees and the landscape.

CROSS SECTION

ELEVATION

fundamental issues of the occupation of site and space. The fit to the land and the relationship with the sun, view and breeze are thoughtfully considered and exploited to enhance the qualities of each scheme. A respect for the lessons of Queensland's traditional architecture is evident in most projects in the layering of the edge condition, the adoption of straightforward construction techniques and materials and in the employment of disciplined planning strategies.' While the Clares are aware that their practice is often referred to as regional, they believe that their work also embodies universal values and themes that extend its relevance beyond local concerns.

COTTON TREE PILOT HOUSING

Extended rooflines and lightly framed window shades maintain sun control while internal breezeways channel cooling air through the interiors of the three-storey buildings.

COTTON TREE PILOT HOUSING

The buildings draw on the pre-existing local language of simple beach houses and sloping-roofed skillions (outhouses or shacks). Variation in street width and length creates public squares or parking courts. Curved streets serve to calm vehicular traffic.

CROSS SECTION

SKI AND SKURF

The Ski and Skurf tourist park is situated on a narrow spit of land between two lakes. Its lightweight structure is clad in plywood, fibre-cement sheet, polycarbonate sheet and corrugated zincalume sheets under an undulating set of roof forms.

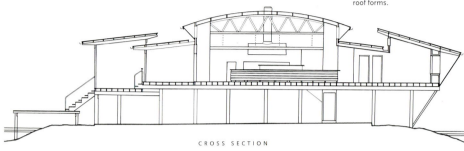

CROSS SECTION

SOFTWARE RITUALS OF THE CONTEMPORARY ASIAN CITY OR HOW TO READ ASIAN CITIES

AKIRA SUZUKI TRANSLATION BY KEITH VINCENT

Over the course of only a few years in the latter half of the twentieth century the cities of South-east Asia have experienced explosive development. Economic expansion has led directly to urban expansion, and investments from outside have continually spurred construction and urban concentration. In the past these cities were characterized by low-level, high-density residences, outdoor markets, the heat of the climate and the spontaneous activity of the masses. But this is not the Asia that has attracted the attention of the architects who have begun to flood there in recent years. For them it is a place with more than enough space and capital to support skyscrapers – a place where loose regulations make all kinds of architecture possible and where every architect can realize his or her vision. The mosaic-like pattern of tropical forests and monsoons, shabby wooden settlements, street markets and canals, on which efforts at urban planning were superimposed by former colonial powers – the entire 'climate' of the city – is to be cleared away or relegated to the periphery of the new city dreamed of by these architects. Asia is attracting not only architects looking for a good business venture but also theorists of the city wanting to experience at first hand the trajectory of these explosive transformations.

But have we not faced this kind of phenomenon before in our own environments? Have we forgotten, for instance, projects like the waterfront and convention-city development in Japan or the 1980s development boom in the US and Europe? Of course the scale of the current boom in Asia greatly exceeds that of the 1980s. Whether in London or Tokyo, this kind of runaway development was doomed to fail from the outset. The present drive to urbanization does not permit easy predictions, and the matter is complicated by factors such as the currency crisis that is afflicting Malaysia and elsewhere. The demand for new urban structures may consist of nothing more than speculation on future demand, which it is hoped will emerge as a result of current construction. Already a great number of massive skyscrapers are being built. Will the desperate scramble for tenants once they are built continue, such as happened in Shanghai in late 1997? And what of the competition that will arise when several massive cities grow up straddling national borders? Will the potential markets of Asia be able to provide enough demand to support these enormous cities? And yet, as if to quell these doubts, the struggle to attract capital continues apace (much of it coming from ethnic Chinese living abroad). In order to emulate the success of such places as Singapore and Hong Kong, the cities of South-east Asia have to attract more business and continue to create more new urban centres as fast as they can be built – all this activity resulting from the extraordinary pace of social change, which far exceeds the control of traditional urban planners.

Surely it is right now to regard Asia's cities as cities rather evidence of changes which markets, and to star we architects. urba

I propose that we think of this extraordinary pace of change as the defining characteristic of urban expansion in Asia today. Hong Kong's Kowloon Walled City is a useful example. The Kowloon Walled City experienced a great influx of refugees after the Chinese Revolution, creating a great demand for housing and bringing about a continual piecemeal extension of its existing high-rise structures. Originally a residential quarter, it eventually developed into what can only be called a city in itself. It was a complex web of connected apartments with few distinguishing architectural features – simple slabs jumbled together like noodles in a bowl of Chinese soup . One could call it a slum but it did not appear entirely random and did have a certain order about it. There was, however, no ordering of space that might have resembled 'urban planning'. Kowloon Walled City had no urban rules in any conventional sense. Only through the necessities of connection and compromise with the structure's continually developing nature could the bare minimum of rules be created to guarantee that inhabitants could manage to walk between the buildings and legal and illegal arrangements evolve for facilities and piping, protruding balconies and antennae on roofs. The whole city took shape out of such provisional adjustments and compromises. I do not find randomness and uncontrolled density aesthetically appealing, but I would argue that this example of order created out of chaos by its users is undeniably a new sort of city. There are of course major differences between the scale and the foundations of the current urban expansion in Asia and this now-extinct squatter's paradise, but I believe that much could be learned from its example.

Architects and their Curiosity Regarding Asian Cities

Architects and urban planners come to Asia with one or more of the following goals: 1) conceiving of ideal or imaginary cities; 2) identifying the problems of actual cities and offering critiques and possible solutions; 3) identifying the deep structures within actual cities and gathering up their fragments; 4) describing the city on the basis of an understanding of those deep structures; 5) comparing a number of cities.

The enthusiastic interest in the cities of Asia that has arisen in the late twentieth century often originates in America and Europe. I am suspicious of it because it seems to me that it projects too many unrevised concepts on to the cities of Asia.

han as
o look for

planners and urban theorists may have not yet perceived?

Many of these ideas arrive as if they were being concocted for a newly discovered continent. Too many architects and urbanists see Asia as virgin territory, which has not yet experienced the retreat of commercial urbanism and the structural demise of traditional urbanism that resulted from the redevelopment of the modern metropolis during the economic boom-and-bust period of the 1980s and early 1990s. Surely it is right now to regard Asia's cities as cities rather than as markets, and to start to look for evidence of changes which we architects, urban planners and urban theorists may have not yet perceived? The actual city is typically divided into constituent parts with the help of structuring concepts such as the oppositions between the city and the village, between downtown and the suburbs, the centre and the margins, or the idea of multilayered communities and infrastructures. But this process is itself inevitably mediated by ideology. In order to avoid this, some choose to limit their focus to extremely small, prescribed regions. Or sometimes the discussion will focus on particular places such as 'suburbia' or 'terrain vague'. There have been several examples of this kind of site-specific urbanism. They have a certain concrete reality. Of course such limited communities are not fixed ones like the suburban neighbourhood. The contemporary city is always fluid, with the user as its object. (Otherwise it would not qualify as a contemporary city.) Identifying proactive significance in negative communities is a way to initiate action towards a new kind of city (this is also the way towards a new urbanism).

Will it be possible to apply individuated concepts of urbanism and the sociology of specific places to an Asian context? One factor is the speed with which Asian cities transform themselves, not only in terms of structures, but also of the users of these cities. Asian cities are already dominated by ephemerality and the speed of communication.

A New Method for Observing Urban Experience

It is an indisputable fact that I live in a city called Tokyo. But when it comes to theorizing about this city there is always the temptation to find a metaphor for the city as a whole and to treat it reductively as an example of the city's structure. Any attempt at reaching an objective perspective is subject to ideological determination. I abandoned this method some time ago in favour of a thoroughgoing effort to find

Whatever the origins of phenomena
once they become visible and such as Tamagotchi,
begin to spread throughout
the city, it become

'things and phenomena that suggest the city' out of a variety of concrete experiences. I try to find new signs of the city within new phenomena and events arising there.

An experiment, Craig Reynolds's 'Boid', may illustrate my position. 'Boid' is a programme which simulates the flight patterns of a flock of birds. Reynolds's initial observations of the flight of a flock of crows led him to believe that the birds were flying as a unit in accordance with a single command, for example to make a formation or perform a sudden turn. He assumed that this was what made it possible to maintain the formation even when an individual bird fell out of the pattern or got separated from group. It proved impossible, however, to find a single crow that seemed to be in control of the whole flock. Eventually he realized that the behaviour of the individual crows was scattered and that they reacted only to the birds in their immediate vicinity. This gave him the idea that it might be possible to create (using artificial birds) a natural flocking movement by prescribing a few simple principles dictating how each crow should react to the birds surrounding it. The following are the three principles he came up with: 1) fly in the direction in which the majority of the neighbouring birds are heading; 2) adjust the speed and direction of flight to that of the closest birds; 3) maintain the appropriate distance to avoid colliding with close-flying birds or other objects.

These principles do not dictate the behaviour of the flock as a whole, that is to say, they are not ideological. Nor do they constitute an order to form a flock. They merely prescribe the nature of mutual relations with the neighbouring crows. The result of the experiment was that the simulated flock of 'boids' exhibited an unexpectedly natural movement. But what surprised Reynolds most was what happened when he had the flock fly into an obstacle. Despite the lack of any specific programming, the flock naturally split down the middle to avoid the object and then came back together. Moreover, the one bird that missed the timing of the turn and ran into the obstacle rejoined the flock after a few seconds of confusion.

This model suggests a way to describe urban phenomena while maintaining a certain distance from the concrete conditions that constitute the city. Could it be applied to the composing of a new image of the city out of its otherwise elusive flows of people and things? Of particular interest is the example of the crow that lost its way. There are always sudden modifications, accidents and instances of play that were not

possible to think of them as models of communication transformed into urban groupware, which contain a new form of communication.

anticipated when the algorithm was written. They have become daily affairs in the contemporary city that we inhabit. The complex behaviour of this lost bird no doubt has hidden within it the signs of a new city. The following are the parameters of the things I would identify as signs appearing in the city:1) phenomena that do not form communities but do constitute coherent groups; 2) networks that may not come together in a specific region or form a neighbourhood but which function as a group; 3) activities that are related purely to communication and not accompanied by traditional infrastructures or economic activities.

The Tamagotchi as Simulacrum of the City

The Tamagotchi is an egg-shaped machine with an electronic clock inside. It is a simulation game in which you raise a chick hatched from an egg, within the space of a tiny liquid-crystal display. Depending on the way it is raised, the chick's appearance changes in unpredictable ways as it grows up. If you don't play with it every day it becomes sluggish and lazy, and if you don't clean up its droppings properly it can

Instead of thinking of communication networks only in terms of hardware, we should now

become ill and die. But the manual for this toy does not contain exact information about how this virtual pet's upbringing will affect it as an adult bird. Judging from the name, the Tamagotchi game was designed to be marketed to high-school-age girls and it is they who have uncovered the mysteries (or secret techniques) of raising a Tamagotchi by way of a vast gossip session conducted over cellular phones and the Internet.

The network of these high-school girls, aged fifteen to eighteen, appears initially to be loosely defined while at the same time extremely exclusive, but it functions as a piece of groupware, returning the fruits of its efforts to the city. The girls are clearly identified by their school uniforms. On their way to and from school they emit signs that make them opinion leaders of fashion and other trends (especially since many private girls' schools are located in central urban areas). Whatever the origins of phenomena such as Tamagotchi, once they become visible and begin to spread throughout the city, it becomes possible to think of them as models of communication transformed into urban groupware, which contain within them the systems and functions of a new form of communication – one very unlike isolated and private systems such as computer game software, comic books or animated films, which forever remain invisible in the cityscape.

Once it became visible, the Tamagotchi boom gave rise to a cacophony of rumours and canards about the sales of the toy. Which supermarket planned to carry it became the subject on everyone's lips and there were stories of toy stores offloading poorly selling toys by packaging them in an embrace with a Tamagotchi. Suddenly the media were abuzz with talk of Tamagotchi thefts, of huge numbers of counterfeit Tamagotchi and of raids on pirate Tamagotchi factories in China. An exclusive urban groupware simulacrum thus became transformed into a series of events related to things and money and even crime. Like the 'boids', the high-school girls were concerned only with the 'boids' next to them, but as a whole they formed an orderly formation.

Rituals of the Contemporary City

In the beginning there is only the shared experience of the Tamagotchi game. This experience itself is a trivial one, lacking the explicit signs of fashion, and also without the physical compensations offered by pop music or amphetamines. It is not necessarily mediated by any economic act. Once it is accelerated, however, it induces events that supersede the mere experience of a game. These are simulated experiences, but when they are shared by many players, accumulated and taken up in repeated communications, their network begins to function and pick up speed. egin to see the city itself as a form of software.

Eventually a communal sensibility emerges. Here we can identify a marvellous movement of a different order from a mere boom or trend. There is no need here for a community or a local unity, for a neighbourhood. Can we not call it an urban experience?

Within the last few years Japanese cities were struck with a natural disaster, the Kobe earthquake, with terrorism, the Aum Shinrikyo subway poisonings, and with a wave of food poisonings in schools. These were incidents unlike any that afflicted local communities of the past. They were entirely mobile experiences shared by large numbers of citizens who happened to be in the wrong place at the wrong time. By a bizarre coincidence, the victims of each of these incidents numbered around five thousand. Moreover, each was a function of urbanization: in the form, respectively, of overpopulation, mass transport systems and school lunch systems. The slightest disturbance to any one of these systems brings disproportionately tragic effects. These incidents may be characterized as passive rituals, in the making of which 'scale' functioned as an important factor. Whether five thousand is a large number compared with the thirty million who live in and around Tokyo, it is certainly large enough, by the rules of probability, for most people to have been directly or indirectly affected, and it was more than large enough to paralyze the infrastructure of the city and to inflict trauma, or the ritualization of trauma, on every last inhabitant. In the Kobe disaster it was not the government or the public authorities but the organized efforts of volunteers that proved most effective in the relief efforts. Urban rituals may be thought of as communication networks close to home and they have proved themselves capable of unimaginable feats, for example, of inflicting sufficient damage to cause the breakdown of an entire city. I stress the idea of urban rituals because I see them as a means of restructuring the city. It is often remarked that communication networks have the capacity to complement urban systems as we have known them hitherto. But perhaps that past tense is a stumbling block. Instead of thinking of communication networks only in terms of hardware, we should now begin to see the city itself as a form of software.

The Urban Rituals of Tokyo

In an urban environment such as Tokyo, which may be neutral but is inevitably fluid, at least in a sociological sense, specific communities organized around a common class, race or region, that is to say, 'neighbourhoods', rarely arise. Instead, we see the emergence of pseudo-communities such as the Tamagotchi girls or communities based on interpersonal relations such as convenience stores. These are artificial communication and distribution systems capable of interacting with various networks without the mediation of the neighbourhood.

Tokyo has been an ideal setting for the development of these kinds of artificial systems, thanks to the concentration in the city of every conceivable type of economic, transport and communication network that could be established in the 1970s and the 1980s – an excessive investment that effected the total destruction of neighbourhoods and communities. The contradictions inherent in this process manifested themselves, for example, in the chaos of Tokyo residential interiors and in the disorder of the cityscape itself.

If one defines the contemporary city in terms of the degree of accumulation and multilayering of infrastructures, Tokyo certainly qualifies. But this kind of multilayering introduces qualitative changes in the city structure. Systems and networks that may at first appear purely artificial and functional can give rise to unimagined complexities which are nothing if not rituals. Such complexities do not emerge from even the most intense concentration of the hard infrastructure but from the acceleration and intricacies of communication. Even a little gadget like the Tamagotchi is enough to create them. Similarly, Tokyo's convenience-store network was created out of a variety of computer inventory and distribution systems, but its attractiveness as a set of meeting places for young people late into the night could not have been inferred from the original algorithm and can only be characterized as ritualistic.

Currently we are experiencing the destabilizing of past urban systems by the direct influence of the new urban infrastructure created within (invisible) communication networks. Inside the bubble of frenzied excitement that Asian cities have inflated in the minds of architects and developers, far vaster and more convoluted urban rituals are being invented by the city's users themselves. They should not be overlooked.

03

DENSE-CITIES / SPRAWL-CITIES
ARCHITECTURE IN THE EXPANDING NEW WORLD CITY

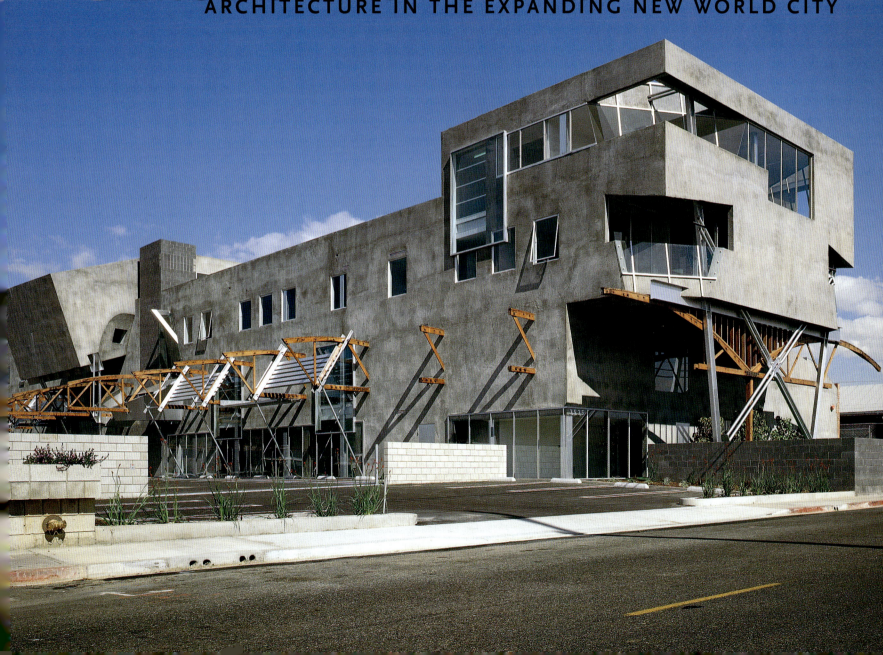

In the five decades following the close of the Second World War, a period marked by the rise of corporate capitalism, transnational manufacturing (the global factory) and the transnationalization of the corporation, the Asia-Pacific region has been massively affected by the processes of modernization and urbanization. If in 1950 the region was for the large part wholly rural and no city on the edge of the Pacific could claim a population of more than five million people, by 1990 ten conurbations on the Rim – Mexico City, Shanghai, Beijing, Seoul, Los Angeles, Jakarta, Tokyo, Manila, Tianjin and Osaka – each already had or was predicted soon to have a population of at least eight million. During this time – a period marked by rapid decolonization – many of the region's traditionally rural subsistence economies were transformed into urban and politically independent commercial economies incorporated within the global political and economic system. Predictions suggest that by 2025 twelve to fifteen cities along the Rim may have populations of ten million or more. Urban transition in the region over the next thirty years will be marked by highly uneven patterns of migration and development that will create metropolitan arrangements and living conditions beyond the horizons of most of today's architects and urbanists.

The worst enemy of modern architecture is the idea of space considered solely in terms of its economic and technical exigencies, indifferent to the ideas of the site …
Vittorio Gregotti, lecture to the New York Architectural League, 1983

Dense-Cities

In some parts of this sphere, especially those still regarded as part of the developing world, the volatile and uneven transnationalization of capital will lead to the creation of regional, superdense and impossibly overpopulated megacities – Mexico City, Jakarta and Shanghai – which will act as powerful magnets, radically emptying rural agricultural areas of their populations with the lure of jobs, housing and access to the global consumer lifestyle. Traditionally rural areas will wilt as their populations and resources are drained. While it is important to distinguish between the cities of Asia, where rapid growth is a relatively new phenomenon, and the cities of Latin America, where levels of urban growth have traditionally been high, these regions will certainly share conditions of massive overpopulation within an often strained social, economic and environmental context. True, these cities will continue to provide many benefits to their inhabitants (easier access to work, healthcare, education, etc.) but they will also present many hazards and discomforts: cramped living conditions, exposure to dangerous pollutants and little or no access to basic utilities and amenities. It is doubtful whether such an excessive model of human existence is even sustainable.

If all of the [world's] urban population lived at a density of 7,600 per square kilometre, which is the average for the major cities of East Asia, then they could be accommodated on less than one per cent of the world's landmass, an area roughly equivalent in size to Germany.
David Clark, *Urban World/Global City*

Sprawl-Cities

The countries of the Asia-Pacific that have followed the late-capitalist model of urban expansion have demonstrated similar patterns of population growth and urban redistribution. The trend in the development in these countries is toward unprecedented sprawling, super-sized settlements – low-density, half-urban/half-rural agglomerations that may measure hundreds of kilometres across. The continuous band of coastal settlements included in the Los Angeles-San Diego-Tijuana nexus is an example of this phenomenon. New mutations in the basic outline of the city are already under way. The low-density, underused, disused or sometimes decaying inner regions of these cities are ringed by unabated, unplanned suburban developments linked by the endless ribbons of the freeway and the information highway. The new city model is based less on traditional civic relationships than on pure consumerism. The elements of this new city – the featureless information factory, the gated community, the commercial franchise, the anonymous strip mall and the tangled parking-lot complexes of the periphery – substitute expediency and get-rich-quick consumerism for durability, permanence and a genuine sense of civic engagement.

The mythical western frontier ... is being transformed into a manufactured landscape, littered with architectural debris ... The resultant implications of this car-dependent, land-consumptive, throw-away culture are appalling ...'
Kelly Shannon, *Sprawl: Colorado's Front-Range*

Architecture in the Expanding New World City

As dire as these predictions for the development of the Asia-Pacific region must seem, they are by no means final or absolute. Strategically planned urban design and architecture will undoubtedly play key roles in tackling unchecked urban development. On the plus side, they have a vital new milieu within which to work. Indeed, it may be that the problems will encourage a new type of urbanism and architecture, a re-engineered approach to citymaking that draws its energy from the dynamic forces at work in the contemporary urban situation. Some architects in the Asian-Pacific sphere have already begun to develop tactical and provocative ways to grapple with these urban changes. Melbourne-based Lyon Architects respond to the commercially expedient and materially insubstanial with careful manipulation of a veneer-thin architecture for the thin, fast cities of the periphery. Eric Owen Moss gathers up the fragmentary disorder of Los Angeles's endlessness into urban collages that evoke the possibilities of a re-engineered City of Angels. TEN Arquitectos are building a remarkably refined yet tough architecture that creates moments of subdued tranquillity in the midst of Mexico City's cacophony. In the heart of Hong Kong's dense urban geography, Michael Tonkin crafts polished, street-smart, super-cool architectural jewels that glow in their hypercompressed settings. Working within Tokyo's seemingly endless urban fields, the Ushida Findlay Partnership, a Japanese-British firm, proposes fluid, geometrically intense, organic architecture that aims to fuse that city with the landscape and perhaps return its inhabitants to a closer relationship with nature. Finally, Malaysian architect Ken Yeang has cultivated an acutely refined, tropical, high-tech architecture, an intelligent option when compared to the numerous, wasteful and misplaced tower developments that define South-east Asia's growing cities. The future cities of the Asia-Pacific Rim will undoubtedly be further impacted by extremely volatile and irregular patterns of growth and migration. The architect-urbanists presented in this chapter have begun to respond to these challenges, but architecture alone will not solve the problem of sprawling growth in the developed world or the threat of urban implosion, which is beginning to present itself in the developing world. Only a determined political and economic effort on the part of government and business may provide the right solutions for the imminent problems.

LYON ARCHITECTS
MELBOURNE, AUSTRALIA

Contriving an architecture of pure surface for the thin and fast cities of Australia

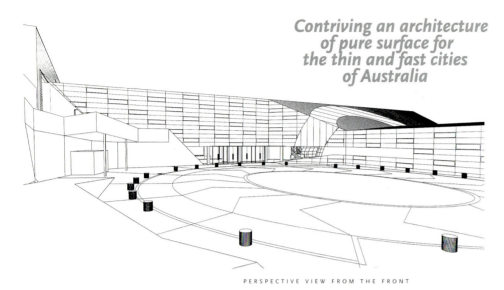

PERSPECTIVE VIEW FROM THE FRONT

BOX HILL INSTITUTE OF TAFE NELSON CAMPUS STAGE ONE

The project involved a two-phase conversion of an existing 1960s warehouse structure into classrooms, a library and auditoria set on a suburban site near Melbourne.

CAREY LYON is interested in the apparent thinness, insubstantiality and expediency of construction in Melbourne's expansive and sprawling periphery. In his treatise of 1993, *Urbanism for a Thin World*, Lyon calls for a city constructed out of postcards rather than concrete – the thin, commodified and ephemeral replacing the deep, authentic and permanent. In the exurbs the curtain wall

BOX HILL INSTITUTE OF TAFE NELSON CAMPUS STAGE ONE

The courtyard features illusionistic shadows in the entry façade and an eye-popping vehicular super-graphic (not shown here).

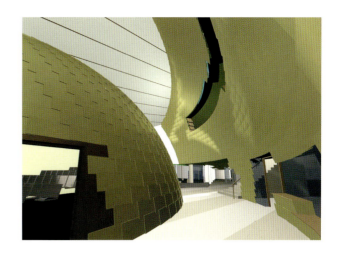

contains the entire civic gesture, Lyon argues. His contemporary city is compressed and embedded in a universal thinness of 150 millimetres of cladding, insulation and structure.

Lyon believes that urbanist-architects have to engage with the contemporary urban environment on its own terms if they are to maintain their relevance and influence over the development of the city. Traditional urbanism is concerned with the infinite complexities and intricacies of an existing historical city, a space built out of accumulated and aggregated forms; it is history layered on history. The traditional urbanist-architect operates within this trenchant historical space, content to add to the layers, building a small piece of the imminent future but respecting the remote past. However, as the city empties its population on to its edges and material production moves to the edges of reality, urban space is finally freed from the outmoded relationship between appearance and content. The city is transformed into another kind of space: one defined not so much by formal consistency as by the informal gaps and

BOX HILL INSTITUTE OF TAFE NELSON CAMPUS STAGE ONE

Plans for the campus building include the introduction of another auditorium (ABOVE) and the completion of the rear half of the development (BELOW).

BOX HILL INSTITUTE OF TAFE NELSON CAMPUS STAGE TWO

The interior circulation void (ABOVE) resembles an external streetscape stretched thin and pasted hard up against the pre-existing warehouse structure.

PERSPECTIVE VIEW FROM THE REAR

interstices of the built landscape and the two-dimensional and deep surfaces of the highway and the mall. For Lyon this new type of city presents an opportunity to produce an architecture that is neither a form of critical analysis nor a search for any deep structures, but rather an attempt to get under the periphery's skin, uncovering 'some modest half-truths'; a dim light flickering over the surface of contemporary urbanism. Lyon's recent project for the Box Hill Institute of Tertiary and Further Education (TAFE) exemplifies this approach. The project involved a two-phase conversion of an existing 1960s warehouse structure into classrooms, a library and auditoria set on a suburban site some forty minutes' drive east of central Melbourne. Lyon explores 'thin-space' in this project through a variety of surface deformations and spatio-graphical experiments. Like his other buildings for educational institutions, notably the Sunshine Campus of the Western Hospital Institute of Tertiary and Further Education, the Box Hill project builds material thinness and the thinness of the image, employing illusory veneers, cladding patterns and floor surfacings in a series of graphical experiments.

SUNSHINE CAMPUS WESTERN HOSPITAL INSTITUTE OF TAFE

The paper-thin entry-face graphic held up by this spacious structure can be seen in this side elevation (ABOVE). A large mushroom-like canopy that makes an oblique reference to roadside petrol stations projects out of the primary façade to mark the entry (RIGHT).

RMIT UNIVERSITY SWANSTON
SPORTS HEALTH AND
EDUCATION BUILDING

The central 'tube' (LEFT) is deftly cut
at its intersection with the street.
The interior sporting space (BELOW)
resembles the inside of some
vast marine vessel.

Lyon believes that in the periphery public architecture is not
actually disappearing – instead it is thinning, spreading out its
volume to allow surface area to develop into a two-dimensional
panorama full of potential civic life. Indeed, Lyon posits that the
curtain wall's 150 millimetres is 'the full depth of deepest
urbanism … the City of Commerce as Pure Architecture'.

RMIT UNIVERSITY SWANSTON
SPORTS HEALTH AND
EDUCATION BUILDING

This project for a university sports
facility in central Melbourne wraps
its vast programme in a large metal
wormlike volume that twists
around its complex site.

ERIC OWEN MOSS
LOS ANGELES, USA

A Los Angeles iconoclast builds fragmentary treasures in a city of multiple and shifting truths

LOS ANGELES is a place where ugliness is only skin-deep, where even death can be cured and pathos means ethos. Los Angeles is a city in which contradictions can be pursued as if they were truths and the whole may be captured in the part or vice versa. Working from his base in Culver City, within the mammoth urban agglomeration known as greater Los Angeles, Eric Owen Moss has refined an ambition, an admissible desire, to remould that city in its own image; or, better, to decant its unusual essence into his own characteristic brand of architecture. That might seem like an implausible challenge, to capture or freeze-frame Los Angeles – a city of contradictions, an almost undefinable entity – in a recognizable form. In Los Angeles, Moss says, '... everything moves, sometimes violently, sometimes imperceptibly ... The job is to look straight at it. Put down what you see. Don't run ... ' Therein lies a conflict – how to present the truth or perhaps just a truth about a city that sometimes tells only lies about itself. Moss mines these inexorable tensions, fuses L.A.'s oppositions into new, incomplete wholes/holes; he balances between the perishable and the permanent in a city he has termed 'the all at once'.

Samitaur, part of a series of developments that the architect has undertaken in the Culver City area with Frederick Smith, a developer of great vision and foresight, is one example of Moss's efforts to retool L.A., to sustain a fragile,

SAMITAUR

Steel legs lift the bulk of the building over the site allowing it to occupy its 'air-rights' allotment fully. Computer-generated studies depict the project as a massive block lifted by regular steel legs over a pre-existing nine-metre-wide road. Two primary anomalies in the building, a south-oriented court and staircase and a north-facing pool, fountain, bridge and seating area over the main entry point, are carved out of the longer block.

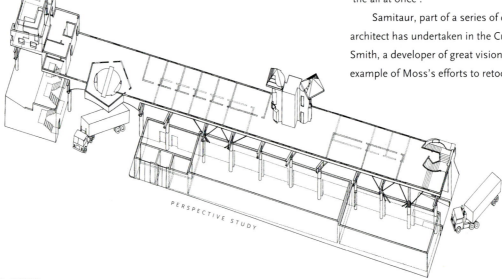

PERSPECTIVE STUDY

The elevated court and staircase configuration for the complex vaguely recall an hourglass form – radically deformed by Moss's interest in incomplete geometries, including intersecting cone forms.

THE BOX

The Box is a meeting space that was formerly a warehouse building in Culver City, California.

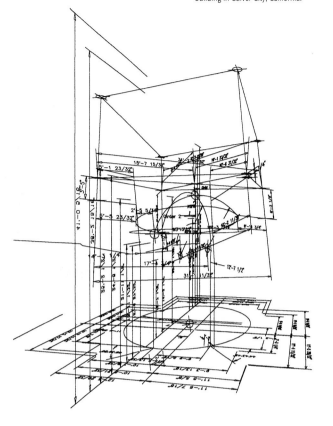

THE BOX

The Box is finished in a uniform surface render that makes no distinctions between roof and wall, interior and exterior.

precarious dance between order and disorder. The project involved the reconstitution of some 9,000 square metres of existing warehouses and the addition of a new office building and conference centre. The new building, the first substantial office construction in the area since the 1992 riots, is over a hundred metres long – a two-storey 'air-rights' office block that is lifted over a pre-existing road. This green-grey hulk sits on a set of steel legs that appear to be placed haphazardly but in fact allow the existing buildings to continue to operate as before. At the southern end of the block a court and stair unit have been carved out of its mass and to the north a double-height conference space is cantilevered over a remodelled, saw-tooth warehouse. Samitaur is the first of three such developments in the area, the last of which will literally hollow out a collection of dilapidated warehouses in the form of a hook shape so that a new building may inhabit the hollow, much as a hermit crab inhabits its shell. Here again, Moss will attempt to build a new incompleteness, a bridge of sorts between a city of no limits and the limits of architecture.

As Moss explains, 'L.A. is without method. Its inability to validate is its strength. L.A. doesn't inculcate value; L.A. doesn't make sense.' The true challenge for Moss has been to build this instability, to resolve the unresolvable unreasonableness of a city that refuses to conform to any known models of urbanity. He has succeeded, creating a series of buildings that are neither jewels nor junk but a much happier resolution – fragmentary treasures.

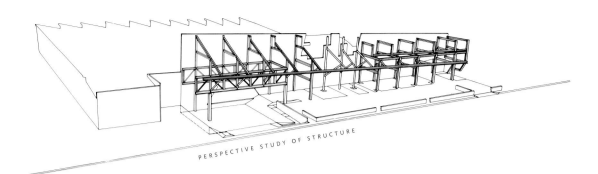

PERSPECTIVE STUDY OF STRUCTURE

STEALTH

This project is wrapped in mystery – it is a three-sided building at one end that magically transforms into a four sided building at the other end. True to its name, the building appears to be constantly moving, never quite still and never totally comprehensible.

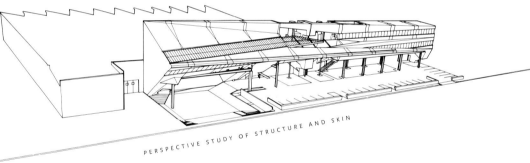

PERSPECTIVE STUDY OF STRUCTURE AND SKIN

BEEHIVE

This project provides a large conference space for an earlier project designed by Moss. Access to the space is from stairs that continue up and around the curving volume to form the roof.

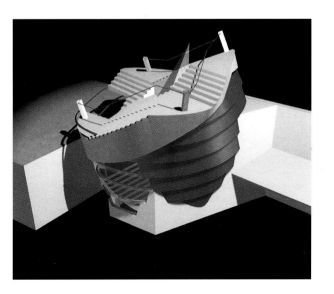

PITTARD SULLIVAN

Designed as the corporate headquarters of a video and computer graphics company, this project involved the renovation and extension of an existing Culver City warehouse. The building combines conventional office space with editing, design and promotional facilities in a dense reworking of the original post-and-bowstring-truss warehouse structure.

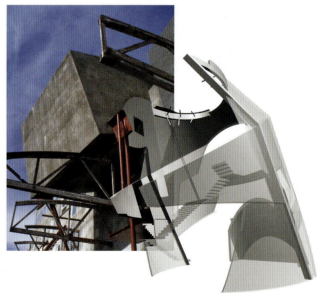

PITTARD SULLIVAN

Moss's additions to the primary structure include a forest of steel columns and wide-flange beams, circulation spaces and four new office towers to the north of the main structure.

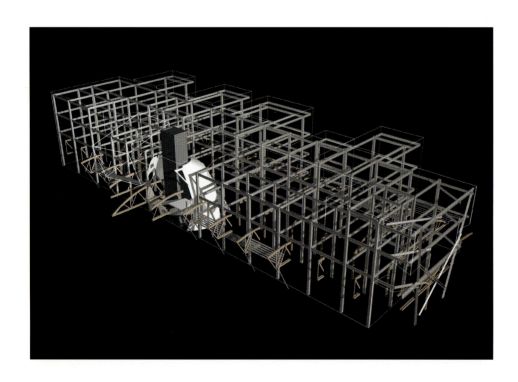

PITTARD SULLIVAN

A series of controlled internal geometric eruptions (RIGHT) serve as public meeting points. Steel bridges and stairs connect the north-facing wings that contain executive offices (BELOW).

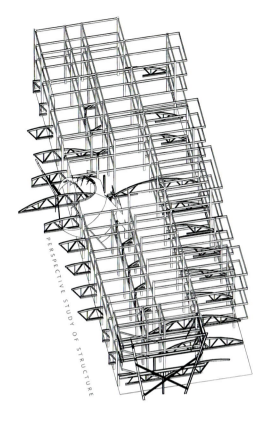

PERSPECTIVE STUDY OF STRUCTURE

TEN ARQUITECTOS

MEXICO CITY, MEXICO

DRAMA CENTER

The exterior eastern façade, which is clad with unfinished Travertine marble, faces a plaza covered with lava rock tiles.

Creating cool, studied landmarks in a mega-metropolis spinning towards an unknown future

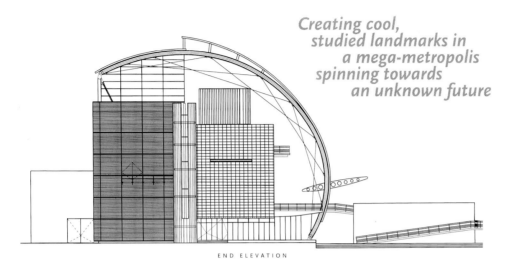

END ELEVATION

TALLER DE ENRIQUE Norten Arquitectos has been responsible for some of the most daring works of contemporary Mexican architecture in the last decade. It was founded in Mexico City in 1986 by Enrique Norton, who had studied both at the Universidad Iberoamericana and at Cornell University. TEN is creating works of architecture that are decided at the point where the vectors of tradition, technologized change and an expansive urban

DRAMA CENTER

The Drama Center's shell form responds to the functional requirements while clearly marking out the building in its busy urban surroundings.

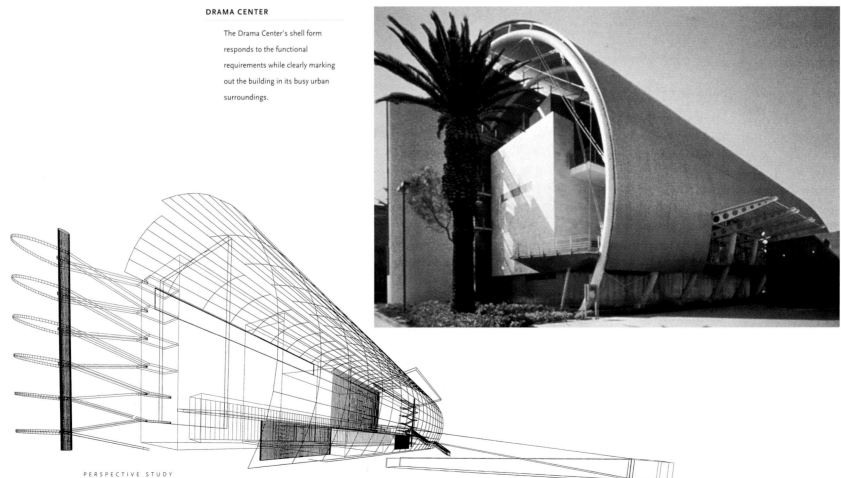

PERSPECTIVE STUDY

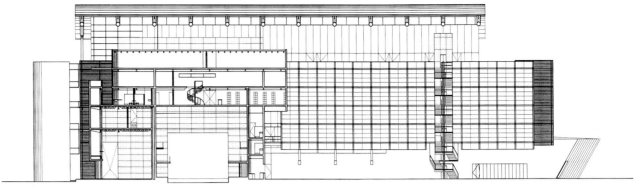

context intersect. In particular, TEN's projects confidently assert themselves in the context of Mexico's almost unimaginably sprawling capital, taking their cue as much from the traditional forms of modern Mexican architecture as from the complexities of contemporary Mexico City. As critic Sylvia Lavin has noted, TEN is a firm '… in the process of reinventing the idea of Mexican Modernism … It explores the contradictions within Modernism that … have not receded into historical memory but continue to operate in the complex production of an ongoing and playfully Mexican modernity.'

TEN Arquitectos's Drama Center in Mexico City, part of Mexico's National Center of the Arts, deals with a difficult combination of contextual conditions with great aplomb. Squeezed between two perpendicular highways linked by a circular ramp in front of the site, and passed by a 'Metro' line, the Drama Center is pounded by continuous competing traffic forces and movements. The site is, moreover, an awkward triangular corner on the extreme north-western tip of the campus

DRAMA CENTER

The external impression of this urban-scaled icon is entirely abstract.

DRAMA CENTER

The distinctive metal-clad extruded shell is supported by a series of curved steel tubes held in tension by steel cables.

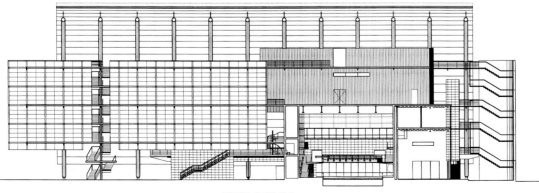

CROSS SECTION

HOUSE LE

Circulation spaces opening on to the south-facing courtyard contain contrasting oak surfaces and an exposed steel structure.

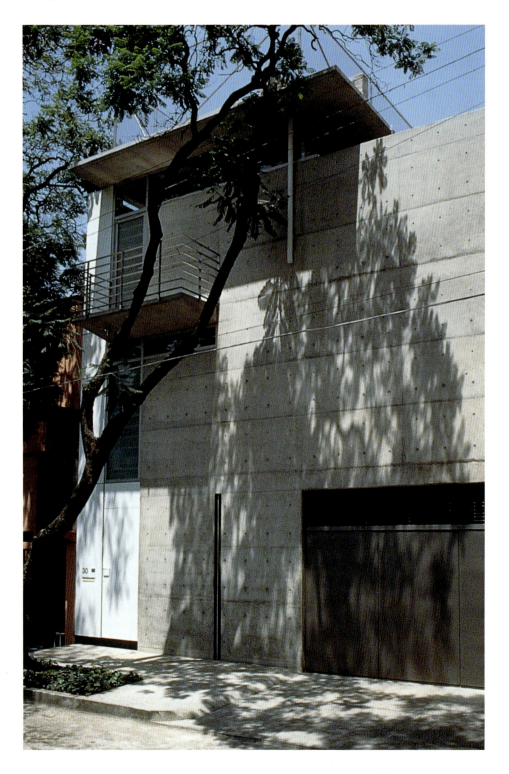

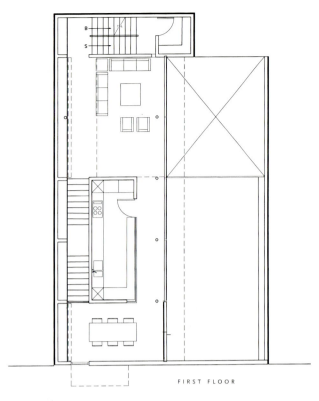

FIRST FLOOR

grounds. The programme called for the accommodation of diverse yet interdependent needs: three performance areas and their support facilities, rehearsal rooms, lecture halls, administration offices, a cafeteria, a gym, scenography studios, costume design labs and a library. TEN designed the project as a series of stacked, individually articulated volumes unified by a common access and meeting space. A form of a shell was generated as an extrusion that could respond to the functional conditions of the main performance space while clearly marking out the Drama Center in its busy urban surroundings.

House Le, a single-family, three-storey residence, is set in Mexico City's Colonia Condesa, a dense, urban residential area primarily made up of townhouses. The site is a 10 x 17-metre lot with a party wall shared with its neighbours. TEN's project is tightly oriented within the extremely confined space. The site was divided in two along its longitudinal axis, creating a concrete living block and an outdoor patio divided by a wall of glazing. The patio has an east-west orientation that provides southern exposure to the house as well as privacy from the street and the neighbouring houses. The principal living, dining and patio spaces are located on the middle floor and connect to the bedrooms above and library below via a stair core at the rear of the house. The ground floor contains the entry, garage, laundry and service bedrooms, while the roof of the house is utilized as a deck. Continuity of materials from exterior to interior suggests

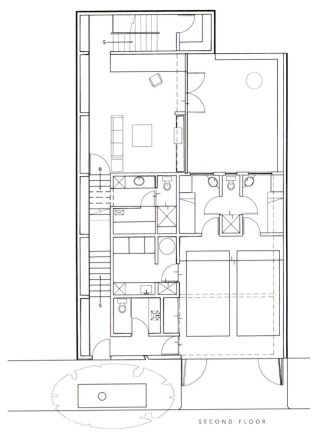

HOUSE LE

The principal living, dining and patio spaces are located on the middle floor, and connect to the bedrooms above and library below via a stair core at the rear of the house.

further spatial transparency between these two zones. The transparencies created by these interlocking volumes provide for various readings of the house and a compact layering of spaces that alludes to Mexico's city's incredible density.

Taller Enrique Norton's projects create powerful and moving spaces in the Mexican capital, landmarks in an uncontrollably spreading city. Yet TEN's architecture is by no means singular or simply monolithic; it is at times reductive and cool and at other moments excessive and expressive. It speaks of the spatial contradictions of the Mexican megalopolis, continuous and undefined, unique and specific, but at the same time marks out new special cultural and physical conditions and terrains.

MUSEUM OF SCIENCES

This carefully proposed building has to maintain the quality and flavour of one of Mexico's City's largest and most important parks while creating over 50,000 square feet of exhibition space.

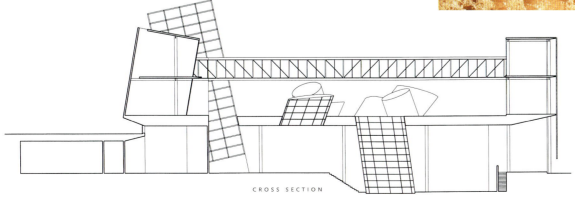

CROSS SECTION

T.R. HAMZAH & YEANG
SELANGOR, MALAYSIA

MENARA MESINIAGA

The Menara Mesiniaga IBM office
tower in Kuala Lumpur combines
environmental sensitivity,
compositional wizardry and a
fine use of the vernacular.

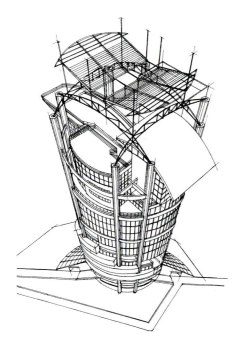

*Cultivating an
acutely refined
tropical high-tech
architecture*

MENARA MESINIAGA

The louvre-shaded sun roof
provides a skeletal framework for
the addition of photovoltaic cells.

IN 1972, WHEN Ken Yeang completed his PhD thesis at Cambridge University he argued 'that there is at present no central theory nor commonly acceptable concept as to what is ecological architecture. If we consider the already extensive and sometimes devastating influences that … our urbanization process has on our natural environment … it becomes apparent that such a theory must be developed.' Today, Yeang is leading the struggle to develop an ecologically sound, sustainable architecture in the midst of South-east Asia's sprawling metropolitan growth. The first step is to stem the tide of environmentally insensitive tower developments. Poorly conceived, with design features that pay lip-service to Asian values, these highly serviced buildings stand in distinct contrast to the series of prototypes Yeang has developed for Asian equatorial cities.

Yeang developed his principles for bioclimatic tropical design in early projects such as the Central Plaza Tower. This is a 35-storey, 30,000-square-metre 'wafer'-thin, column-free structure, which incorporates complex systems of louvres on the hot façades (west-east), planting that diagonally steps up the north face of the tower to reach the pool atrium on the top floor and naturally ventilated and daylit lift-core lobbies, toilets and stairways. Facing north towards the the distant hills of Ampang is a curved, fully glazed curtain wall that allows for views without heat penetration because of its heavy shading.

The Menara Mesiniaga IBM office tower in Kuala Lumpur Yeang lyrically combines environmental sensitivity, compositional wizardry and careful reconsideration of the vernacular uses of natural ventilation, shading and variable skins in the Malaysian building tradition. For this striking 12,000-square-metre tower Yeang developed landscaping and planting mounds which rise up from the ground to spiral up the building into recessed terraces and 'sky-courts', which the designer describes as aerial social condensers for the tower's office-workers. The circular,

TA 2

TA 2 is a mixed-use condominium/
serviced-apartment tower that
provides full solar gain protection
for every unit and will be
fully cross-ventilated.

HITECHNIAGA TOWER

Clad in solar-reflective perforated
sheets, this nineteen-storey tower
will be built on a site about twenty
minutes' drive from the Kuala
Lumpur city centre.

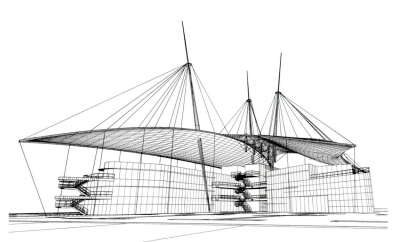

fifteen-storey tower has an intricately figured exterior, which
provides shading, natural ventilation and considerable scope
for daylight penetration to the central core. Along its western
orientation, aluminium screens and shaded sky-courts reduce
heat gain and solar impact. At north and south, maximum
glazing allows filtered daylight to enter. Nearly thirty years after
his doctoral research, Ken Yeang is tackling the catastrophic
urbanization processes with an environmentally responsive and
intensely considered tropical architecture, a reasonable alternative
to the deleteriously designed and misplaced tower developments
that punctuate the skylines of Asia's growing cities.

GUTHRIE PAVILION

This three-storey golf clubhouse
is shaded by a fully independent
pre-tensioned cable, pylon and
pneumatic membrane roof
structure that acts as an
environmental umbrella .

GAMUDA HEADQUARTERS

An elliptical atrium building formed out of two curved office wings. The ten-storey complex incorporates lush green sky-courts, elevated garden terraces and roof gardens.

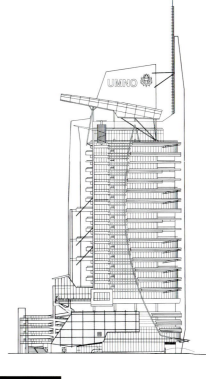

SHANGHAI ARMOURY TOWER

This thirty-six-storey tower will be built in the Pudong district of Shanghai. Landscaped terraces act as lungs for the tower, creating a microclimatic buffer between inside and outside.

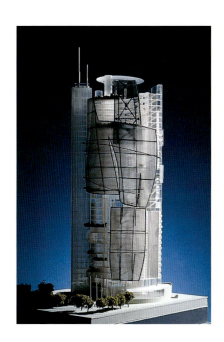

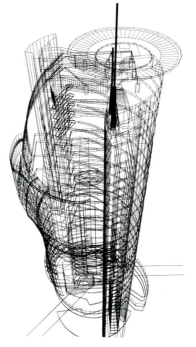

MENARA UMNO PENANG

Menaro UMNO Penang will contain spaces for a banking hall and auditorium as well as twenty-one storeys of office space. Every floor can be naturally ventilated and special wing walls help channel air into the building.

USHIDA FINDLAY PARTNERSHIP
TOKYO, JAPAN

Fusing the city and landscape with a fluid, geometrically intense organic architecture

TRUSS WALL HOUSE

The house makes the most of its small ninety-square-metre plot in exurban Tokyo.

TRUSS WALL HOUSE

The truss wall house exploits the structural possibilities of compound reinforced-concrete construction methods to their fullest in order to produce a pure, seamless and continuously flowing space.

THE USHIDA FINDLAY Partnership is a bi-cultural, ecologically focused architectural team that was formed by Kathryn Findlay (British) and Eisaku Ushida (Japanese) in Tokyo during the mid-1980s. Their practice is dedicated to the fusing of Tokyo's sprawling urban field with the landscape from which it arose. Their projects

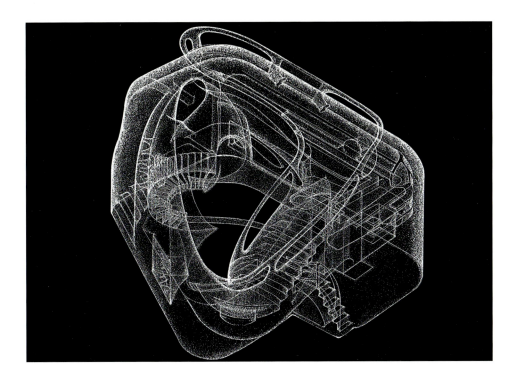

are usually defined by fluid organic geometries that bring the user into a closer relationship with nature. As Riichi Miyake, professor at the Shibaura Institute of Technology, has written, '… in the face of the regrettable hodgepodge of urban environments at the end of the twentieth century, Ushida Findlay propose a combination of architecture and landscape which maximizes the possibilities of the human body and the spirit …'

The strangely beautiful yet thoroughly accomplished Truss Wall House is perhaps Ushida Findlay's best-known project. The client for this project was the concrete contractor for an earlier house, the Echo Chamber. His brief had two aims: first, to exploit his system of compound reinforced-concrete construction and, second, to build a house that would make the most of his small ninety-square-metre plot in exurban Tokyo. Ushida Findlay's solution to these challenges was to exploit the structural qualities of the concrete construction system to produce a pure and continuously flowing set of spaces – a continuity between inside and outside, which would increase the spaciousness of the site by wrapping it into itself. The architects treated the house as a solid blob of frozen space – a vessel form within which a series of topological 'organs' could be massaged into programmatic functionality without a readily comprehensible internal scale. Voided routes formed links and the transition between floor, wall and ceiling was smoothed into an unarticulated, maximized cocooning envelope.

The Soft and Hairy was designed by Ushida Findlay for a young couple who had read that Salvador Dali said the

TRUSS WALL HOUSE

To reinforce the links between internal spaces in the house, the transition between floor wall and ceiling was smoothed into an unarticulated, maximized cocooning envelope.

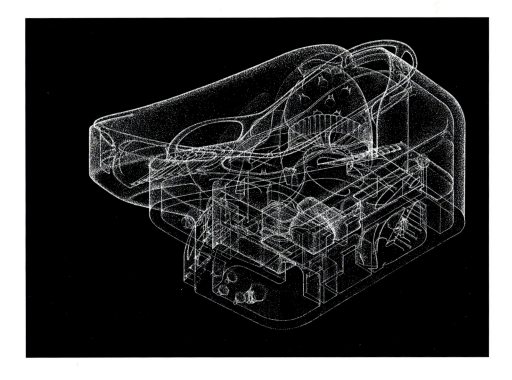

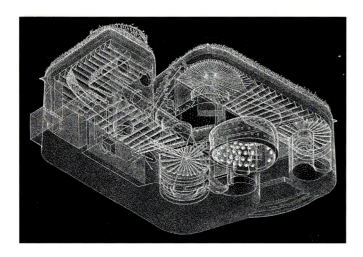

architecture of the future should be 'soft and hairy'. The house, in the Tsukuba New Science City, a housing development on the outskirts of Tokyo, is essentially a large room with sub-rooms facing on to a central courtyard. On either side of the living room two spiral 'caves' form a habitable landscape that evades the realities of the dreary housing development outside. In a poetic gesture seemingly borrowed from Dalí's Surrealist repertoire, Ushida Findlay transferred the original landscape – cut away by the house – to the roof.

Kaizankyo, a company resort in an inaccessible part of Wakayama Prefecture, is nestled between the bases of two

SOFT AND HAIRY HOUSE

The house, in the Tsukuba New Science City, a housing development on the outskirts of Tokyo, is essentially a large room with sub-rooms facing on to a central courtyard.

SOFT AND HAIRY HOUSE

The bathroom has a Surrealist quality reminiscent of Dalí's work.

KAIZANKYO

The resort's community of buildings
is made up of a series of ship-
shaped or leaf-shaped timber
structures.

cedar-covered mountains that look out on to a small inlet of the
Pacific. The resort's community of buildings is made up of a
series of ship-shaped or leaf-shaped structures, which describe a
proportional scale that recalls the chaos geometry first elucidated
by scientists Mandelbrot and Julia. The main house, the
swimming pool, sauna and a small bench spiral along and down
this scaling arm, demonstrating Ushida Findlay's interest in using
fractal structures – hierarchies in which successive levels are
geometrically similar – as a means of echoing nature, in which
these self-referential patterns often occur.

KAIZANKYO

Kaizankyo is a company resort in
an inaccessible part of Wakayama
Prefecture. It nestles between
the bases of two cedar-covered
mountains that look out on to
a small inlet of the Pacific.

ECHO CHAMBER

This residence was designed to resemble a courtyard structure (RIGHT and BELOW) despite a local restriction requiring a deep perimeter strip around the site. Instead the architects have devised a timber box with double-thick flanking walls. The bathroom (OPPOSITE) is a richly textured, soft environment that prophesied later projects like the Truss Wall House.

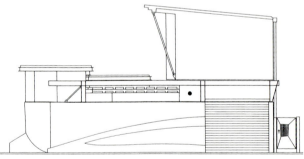

ELEVATION

The Ushida Findlay Partnership argues that the accepted modes of urban composition and the social systems that have traditionally supported architecture are no longer in synchronicity with the contemporary city. Architects, they suggest, can no longer properly address the demands of a rapidly changing society without the invention of a more open-ended spatial discipline. Their stated goal has been to break down the stock responses to the city; and these startling and unusual architectural projects, like some peculiar fruit born of intense genetic manipulation, are cultivated by Ushida Findlay to cause discussion and perhaps even dissent – but never complacency.

MICHAEL TONKIN HONG KONG

Crafting super-cool architectural jewels that glow in Hong Kong's hyper-compressed setting

CONCEPT DRAWING

FONT WORKS

This design for an electronic calligraphy house explores the line between two- and three-dimensional space and the significance of the ancient art of Chinese calligraphy in the contemporary world.

'BEAUTY FOR ME is cheapness', says British-trained, Hong Kong-domiciled architect and designer Michael Tonkin. Whether he's scouring little Kowloon stores for nine-dollar-per-yard pigskin, salvaging fittings from old Hong Kong houses or cutting down and welding the sort of steel plate normally associated with industrial refrigeration units, Michael Tonkin is one architect who appreciates the value of recycling and of street theatre. Indeed, while visitors usually regard the dramatic landscape and the profusion of neon as the most extraordinary features of the former colony, for Tonkin Hong Kong is also a super-dense, if overcrowded, repository of materials and ideas that possess seemingly endless possibilities.

Tonkin's design for the first restaurant to open in the newly developed Quarry Bay is characteristic of his approach to spacemaking. The existing space was converted from six separate car-maintenance workshops into an illusionistically open stage. The disparate and disjointed spaces were effectively united by the use of mirrors, which heighten the diagonal views through the space. The ceiling, an inverted and miniaturized replication of Hong Kong's undulating landscape, further interconnects the former car workshops by leading the eye on a sculpturally swirling dance through the restaurant's dining spaces. In between the columns of the café obscured glass hides another rhythm – a zigzagging pattern of coloured neon tubes. Linked to a computer programme, these recycled nighclub lights pass though various cycles, gradually changing the colour and mood of the space.

The Stanley House, an extensive renovation of an existing 1950s structure, is situated on top of a cliff in the Hong Kong village of Stanley. Tonkin's remodelling dramatically transformed the old structure into a triparite composition that refers to nature, the city and cultural heritage. Composed of a pure white cube facing the sea, a black shell turned away from street and a striking red tower lodged between sea and land, the house is a clean-cut,

Q RESTAURANT

The ceiling, an inverted and miniaturized replication of Hong Kong's undulating landscape, leads the eye on a sculpturally swirling dance through the restaurant's dining spaces.

Situated on the top of a cliff above its own beach, in the Hong Kong village of Stanley, the house is an extensive remodelling of a 1950s structure.

STANLEY HOUSE

Composed of a pure white cube facing the sea, a black shell turned away from the street and a striking red tower lodged between sea and land, the house is a clean-cut, voided structure in an overfull city.

STANLEY HOUSE

A simple cantilevered stone slab (ABOVE) marks the fireplace. The pared-down bathroom (RIGHT) offers magnificent views of the Hong Kong waterfront.

OSCARS

A wall of backlit bottles acts as a
huge sign, a powerful decorative
element and a menu for this mall-
enclosed restaurant.

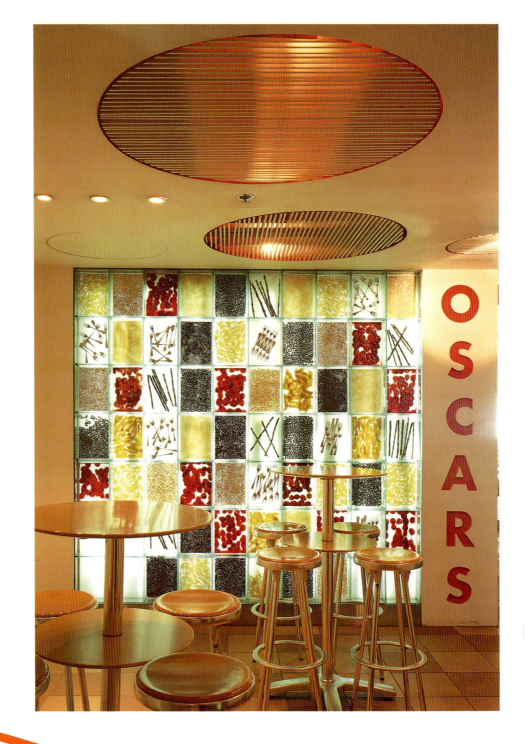

voided structure in a city overfull of densely packed flats and
crowded streets. Space flows diagonally through the house both
in plan and in section, connecting the central living floor with the
bedrooms upstairs and the recreation floor downstairs. As well
as connecting the house spatially, these voids also encourage a
free flow of air to ventilate the house naturally. A play is set up
between the flow of the open plan and the clear assertion of each
room as a separate, non-dependent space. Rooms are entered
and left through thick walls that house storage and services,
lending a sense of solidity and weight to the diagonally connected
chambers. The only feature of the original house retained was a
mahogany handrail. Having stripped every wall, Tonkin then
pieced the house back together with materials salvaged from
old Hong Kong houses and the reclamation yards of England.

Working from his base close to Hong Kong's super-dense
core, Michael Tonkin is a young architect whose crafted, street-
smart and super-cool projects belie their often recycled, salvage-
yard origins. His work transmutes the physical fragments and
discarded dreams of the city into a new and vigorously
retooled environment.

OSCARS

A computer-generated diagram
reveals the restaurant's minimal
but effective design.

PERIMETER POLITICS
THE RIM AND THE BASIN
DAVINA JACKSON

One and a half centuries before the Big Bang theory was proposed, Charles Darwin's grandfather Erasmus (an English doctor and inventor) suggested the explosive origins of the cosmos in a poem, which is also relevant to those interested in considering the significance of what has been termed 'the new Pacific century'.

Writing in 1789, twenty years after James Cook's antipodean voyages, Erasmus described God proclaiming 'let there be light' and triggering stupendous blasts, which shattered the universe into a million suns orbited by earths, from which secondary planets 'issue from the first'. One of Erasmus's secondary planets was our moon: flung heavenward to leave behind a 'wounded side' in 'Earth's huge sphere' … 'where now the South Sea heaves its waste of tide'. Although this dismal word-picture has since been contradicted by paintings and tourist photos showing idyllic palm beaches, Erasmus's conception of the Pacific as a vast basin of brackish fluid still influences our interpretations of the region. His description of the Pacific as a wound in the Earth's surface also underlies current understandings of 'the Pacific Basin' as an unfathomably deep space which strings around itself a glittering necklace of progressive cities linked not by similar cultures or histories but by other factors. They are all located on the dark, 'other' side of the planet from Europe. The same ocean washes their shores. And, most significantly, they all are jostling to promote strong economic relationships with (or within) Asia.

Are those points significant enough to claim a distinct identity for the Pacific's periphery? The rationale looks fragile. In most assumptions, a rim is defined by the

entity it encloses. On this basis, the Pacific's edge cities could forge a sense of
common character only by developing a mutual orientation towards the 'void' that
they surround: an area amounting to almost one-third of the planet's suface area.
Yet such a cultural concentration seems unlikely to happen because the region's
economies are being driven by networks of entrepreneurs who show scant interest
in wooing islands which are not populous, prosperous or strategically significant.
In turn, the central Pacific's cultures of uncomplicated self-sustenance don't seem
obviously compatible with the all-go agendas of contemporary Asia, America and
Australasia.

traditional village buildings On Polynesian islands
do not often appear architectura

Those contradictions are tacitly acknowledged in the list of countries that
participate in the forum for Asia Pacific Economic Cooperation (APEC). Alongside
eleven Asian and four American nations, the only Oceanic countries included in
the group are Australia, New Zealand and Papua New Guinea. Off the list are Tonga,
Fiji, Vanuatu, Kiribati, Tuvalu, Nauru, the Solomon Islands, the Carolines, the
Marianas and the Gilberts – all self-governed – and a variety of atolls and archipelagos
supervised by France, the United States, Australia, Japan, New Zealand, the United
Kingdom and Chile. Also not part of APEC is the former Soviet Union, which has a
Pacific coastline about as long as China's – yet (like Peru and Chile) it is often cropped
off Pacific maps and mentalities. Another difficulty with various scenarios describing
a Pacific Rim condition is that the perimeter cities are inherently schizophrenic.
While sharing the shores of a large body of water, they are also on the edges of
different land masses and inside the borders of countries that compete with each
other for international funds. In theory, such interstitial conditions could trigger
exciting creative tensions in many realms of cultural production, but in fact very few
of the rim's culture producers perceive tangible advantages from focusing on the
Pacific, either as a source of inspiration or as a site to deliver output.

One contrast between the Pacific's centre and perimeter nodes appears in the
different perceptions of the ocean between the cultures of the central Pacific and its
edges. Many cities on the edges of Pacific continents do not seem to have as deep a
consciousness of the sea as they do of their land; even though their histories include
notable marine achievements and they may have strong affinities with local beaches.

However, island people, with limited land to cultivate, have a long record of casting off in search of food, women, war and new places to live.

It is no coincidence that the indigenous people of Hawaii are called 'Maoli', in Tahiti 'Maohi' and in Aotearoa (New Zealand) 'Maori'. Early Polynesians and Melanesians, navigating by the stars, winds, waves and behaviour of sea birds, sailed their canoes all over the Pacific region and are understood to have landed in Madagascar at least a millennium before the Spaniard Vasco Núñez de Balboa reached the Pacific in 1513. Today, the only advanced nations on the rim that sustain strong oceanic instincts are also islands: New Zealand (current holders of the America's Cup) and the Asian nations of Japan and Taiwan (whose trawlers drift-net the sea between both poles). China's coastal cities also have a vigorous maritime background.

n the European sense of having been designed to monumentalize a powerful aspect of the culture.

All the central Pacific islands have been inspected, digested and sometimes dissected by nations on the rim. After four centuries of visits by European explorers, armies from 'Great Turtle Island' (North America) occupied many Polynesian islands during and after the Second World War – and the rusted hulks of armoured vehicles are often pointed out to modern tourists as landmarks. As other examples, Peru snatched several thousand slaves from Tahiti before it became a French protectorate in 1834 and, later in the nineteenth century, Australia's colonists took boatloads of natives from Papua and Indonesia in 'blackbirding' expeditions to stock their properties with labour. Despite (or because of) regular contact with foreign powers, there is a sensitivity in the islands that their ocean is, as Zohl Dé Ishtar wrote in *Daughters of the Pacific* (1994), 'ringed by a deafening silence'. While the rim nations regard the Pacific as a relatively empty (unpopulated) expanse, Dé Ishtar's flipside perception reads the rim as a wall of ignorance and indifference to horrific acts of plunder, murder and nuclear sabotage, justified by often racist rationales.

Other contrasts between the rim and the centre arise from different perceptions of space, time and architecture. But there are significant exceptions to every generalization, and some cultures on the rim share important ideas with communities in the centre. As well, all Pacific societies have different, fragile balances between their building traditions, architectural concepts imported by their invaders and the iconic images now disseminated by American films and television. Any attempt to define a Pacific architecture is doomed by diversity. Nevertheless, some random observations of the region's contrasts may be illuminating.

Australia's Aborigines have never had a need for architecture as Europeans and Asians might understand it. As nomadic hunter-gatherers in a mainly warm climate, they weather-protected themselves by smearing their skins with botanical unguents, and they slept in caves or under shards of bark held up by the branches of eucalypts. For them, 'home' is still understood as an expansive territory, possessed by tribes rather than individual people, and occupied on seasonal walkabouts inspired by songlines from the Dreamtime.

On Polynesian islands, traditional village buildings do not often appear 'architectural' in the European sense of having been designed to monumentalize a

As face-to-face transactions and bureaucratic functions are usurped by telecommunications, Pacific cities are rapidly constructing icons

powerful aspect of the culture. Many villages are regularly destroyed by south-east trade winds and cyclones, but they are also blessed with abundant construction materials from the coconut palm. For these reasons, buildings are understood to have short lifespans. Many are made like the Caribbean huts that fascinated German architect Gottfried Semper in the mid-nineteenth century: frames of poles clad with leaves and branches woven according to particular village techniques.

In Melanesia and Indonesia, societies are often patriarchal, and the architecture of significant community buildings may celebrate male concepts of magnificence with dynamic forms symbolizing thrust, penetration and triumph. Classic examples are the *haus tambaran* – mens' houses – which are the central monuments in villages throughout Papua New Guinea. Entry to these soaring, beaked structures is strictly limited to men (and women tourists with purses to buy crafts stored there). Visitors must climb a ladder to the formal upper hall and step from sunlight to blackness through a doorway surmounted by the carved figure of a spreadlegged female figure.

Less flamboyant than PNG's *haus tambaran*, but in some ways more elaborate, were the *whare whakairo* of the early New Zealand Maori. These single-storey, gable-roofed meeting houses were framed up in native timbers – totara, manuka, rimu or

kauri – and thatched with raupo or toetoe bush. The façades were distinguished by
several unusual features: a generous porch with woven walls interrupted by decorative
panels in red and black patterns; barge-boards elaborately carved at the ends with
spiral patterns inspired by the coiled leaves of ponga ferns; and, on top of the centre
pole, a statue named *koruru*, which an early French explorer once described as 'a
hideous figure, a sort of sea devil'.

These models of traditional South Sea 'architecture' have all been constructed
without architects, a profession that is only now being contemplated by Pacific
Islanders. It is only recently that selected Polynesians, such as Tonga's architect,
George Mulawa, and Fiji's government architect, Cama Tuiloma, have been sent
to Australia and New Zealand to obtain qualifications to help them design and
supervise a new generation of public work.

Australia itself has no indigenous registered architects but has several Aboriginal
graduates, notably Dennis McDonald, who heads the Aboriginal design unit in the
New South Wales government architect's office. He and his peers are being asked to

which have the triple purpose of attracting foreign income entertaining tourists, and catering to the expanding leisure interests of local citizens.

consider how to balance sudden demand for Aboriginal cultural and community
centres (a genre considered good for both 'national reconciliation' and tourism) with
debatable concepts about what 'Aboriginal design' might mean and look like. So far,
the only built propositions have been conceived by white architects – and have
palpably different aesthetics. Contradicting the more or less Modernist schemes of
Glenn Murcutt and Denton Corker Marshall for Aboriginal cultural and community
centres are two romantically organic, Aboriginal cultural centres designed by Gregory
Burgess at the sacred desert site of Uluru (Ayers Rock) and in the Grampian ranges
of western Victoria.

Both of Burgess's buildings appear to creep along the ground with the sinuous
langour of long slugs. Mud-brick walls, daubed with tribal paintings, follow
meandering floor plans; undulating roofs of shingles are interrupted by eye-like

circular openings and hooded slits. Although heavily influenced by European precedents – obviously Antoni Gaudí's installations in Barcelona – Burgess's approach highlights some critical themes of Aboriginal culture and powerfully opposes Modernism's reliance on straight lines, grids, mass-produced materials and plain surfaces. For these reasons, his projects appear to be seductive prototypes for a future 'Aboriginal architecture' that never previously needed to exist. In New Zealand, the best-known Maori architect is Rewi Thompson of Auckland, who has also produced buildings intended to oppose colonial architectural conventions. However, he and other Kiwi practitioners show little general interest in Maori architectural form-making. They are generally inspired by European and American innovations and precedents, although they sometimes embellish their works with Polynesian decorative motifs. Polynesian culture remains an incidental interest for almost all Asia-Pacific architects. Ambitious practices prefer to pursue the trails of Asian money being invested in modern building types that are replacing the colonial monuments delivered across the region during the nineteenth century.

If any architect exemplified an early sensibility for the possibilities of a Pacific Rim culture it woul

As face-to-face transactions and bureaucratic functions are usurped by telecommunications, Pacific cities are rapidly constructing icons, which have the triple purpose of entertaining tourists, attracting foreign income and catering to the expanding leisure interests of local citizens. Key genres include the mixed office-residential-retail tower (more sociable and versatile than single-use office blocks and shopping centres); the casino-entertainment-hotel palace (suddenly made legal by the Anglo-Christian cultures of Australia and New Zealand to attract Asian gamblers); museums, galleries and theatres; international convention and trade exhibition centres, often with attached hotels; sports pavilions; and university facilities (to woo Asia's emerging middle classes). Since the Second World War, all Asia-Pacific cities have been visually transformed by glass and concrete commercial buildings modelled on American skyscrapers. In height, these range from a typical two storeys in Vanuatu's Port Vila to the 108-storey Nina Tower now being built in Hong Kong. Constantly thirsting for power to sustain their cool-air systems, these wasteful works may be gradually replaced by more appropriate towers for the tropics: naturally ventilated, sun-responsive, computer-supervised skyscrapers advancing the 'bioclimatic' prototypes already built by Malaysia's Ken Yeang. While international-style high-rises continue to define the region's cities, a contradictory trend is appearing in the architecture of tourist resorts. Reacting against a thirty-year phase of high-rise beach towns such as Honolulu, Acapulco and Surfers Paradise, developers of resorts in 'getaway' locations are now preferring to build clusters of luxurious one- or two-storey guesthouses designed to exemplify local traditions and materials. There is also increasing demand throughout the region for another architectural model: centres celebrating 'exotic' religions and mythologies. Buddhist groups have built some of the most spectacular examples. One is a glistening, multi-storeyed pagoda beside a main highway south of Sydney, designed by Australian firm Jones Brewster Regan using materials imported from China. Another is a serene retreat on a hill near Wellington, New Zealand, built in local timbers and conceived by architect Hugh Tennent to combine traditional temple-design strategies from several Asian countries.

Crosscultural appropriation and exchange have always been among the architect's most basic instincts. One key example is Jørn Utzon's use of the ancient methods of Chinese temple construction and the platform structure in ancient Mayan

ertainly be Frank Lloyd Wright who built a sequence of residences that helped to inspire entire suburbs in Australia and New Zealand.

monuments in his design for the Sydney Opera House. Today, however, in an age of instant communication and rapid international transport it is possible for certain contemporary architects to deliver their concepts personally to a variety of Pacific cities. For example, many key towers in Singapore's business district were designed by American firms during the 1980s and numerous Australian and US-based 'corporate' practices have satellite offices in China, Malaysia, Indonesia, Thailand, Taiwan and South Korea. In Australia, Tokyo architect Kezuyo Sejima recently won the commission to design a Sydney cinematheque, making history as the first woman without a prominent male partner to design a notable Australian public building . These Pacific crossflows were also anticipated by the occidental and antipodean excursions of the Chicago architects Walter Burley and Marion Mahoney Griffin early this century. In 1911, the Griffins won an international competition to design Australia's new capital city of Canberra: after working in and around Canberrra they then moved north to establish a model suburb in Sydney before setting off to India towards the end of their careers. But, if any architect exemplified an early sensibility for the possibilities of a Pacific Rim culture it would certainly be the Griffins' mentor, Frank Lloyd Wright. Inspired as a student by Japanese art and architecture, he returned his knowledge to that culture with his design for Tokyo's Imperial Hotel. Later he would incorporate Aztec motifs into projects such as the Hollyhock (Barnsdale) House in Los Angeles and would build a sequence of residences that helped to inspire entire suburbs in Australia and New Zealand. Wright also proposed 'mile-high cities' like those now being realized in China, Indonesia and Malaysia. Yet, despite his connections to those diverse bases across the Pacific basin, Wright never imagined the Pacific to have an *axis mundi*. We must recognize in our architectural politic today that the absence of such a focus contradicts the popular construction of a generalized Pacific Rim sensibility.

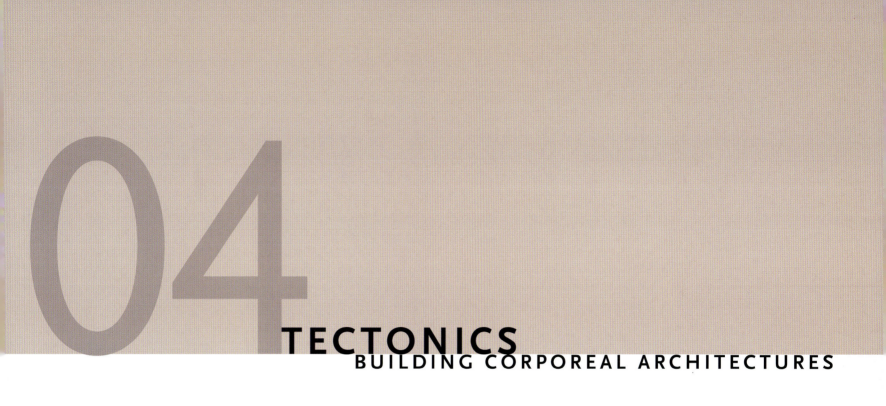

04

TECTONICS
BUILDING CORPOREAL ARCHITECTURES

The tectonic in contemporary architectural culture may be best described as a tendency towards the attentive expression of the material, the structural and the physical in built form. Tectonic architecture favours the tactile over the visual and the spatial over the graphical. It focuses closely on the pleasures of construction, assembly, detail, texture, colour, form and weight. Tectonic architecture concerns itself with the natural qualities and formal properties of constructional materials, the procedures or means of joining constructional elements and the spatio-visual dynamics of form. Common strategies for the production of tectonic architecture combine the deployment of well-considered and refined constructional detailing with an often ductile approach to spacemaking. Usually time-honoured materials are favoured over ordinary or modern components. However, in many instances the discreet and conscientious use of everyday or 'off-the-rack' materials can also be seen as a valid approach to tectonic practice. The physical and the real are both seen as mutually sustaining and primary conceptual and practical territories for creative exploration in tectonic architecture. In some ways this modality of architectural thought and production can be seen as restitution of the phenomenological in architecture; a reparation of time-space of daily existence. Tectonic architecture may also be understood as a reinvigoration of historically appropriate cultural or regional forms by modern means. In this sense it shares many of the concerns of Frampton's Critical Regionalism, namely, careful attention to site conditions, the use of locally available materials and construction methods and a keen sense of economic, political and cultural independence from the forces of market capital. But the tectonic approach should not be referred to as historicist or *retardataire*. It does not forcibly attempt to reclaim historical forms or types and methods of construction because of a sense of nostalgia or loss. Indeed, this very particular architectural operation distinctly breaks away from the Deconstructivist proclivity for non-materially-based investigations of text or subjective meaning and the shallow pop-pastiche of post-Modernist, quasi-historicist semiological architecture. In this sense it is important to emphasize that tectonic architecture does not constitute a stylistic or aesthetic movement. In fact, it is not even a school of thought *per se* but rather an overarching attitude to spatial production that integrates several subtendencies within itself.

To the Greeks téchne *means neither art nor handicraft but rather: to make something appear, within what is present … the Greeks conceived of* téchne, *producing, in terms of letting appear.* Téchne *thus conceived has been concealed in the tectonics of architecture since ancient times.*
Martin Heidegger, *Building, Dwelling, Thinking*

It is undeniable that over the course of the past century the tectonic has assumed a great many forms … Yet one thing persists throughout this entire trajectory, namely, that the presentation and representation of the built as a constructed thing has invariably proved essential to the phenomenological presence of an architectural work and its literal embodiment in form. Kenneth Frampton, *Studies in Tectonic Culture: The Poetics of Construction in Nineteenth and Twentieth Century Architecture*

Corporeal Architecture

Tectonic architecture opens up a field of action for the rebuttal of Lefebvre's assertion. This is exactly because tectonic architecture specifically addresses the way in which the body (and the eye) can be satisfied by a spatial composition. Thus it may be said that fundamentally the tectonic approach generates a corporeal architecture, one in which the body is neither regarded as an abstract energy, a source of flow in the circulation diagrams of some mechanistic design work, nor as an intellectual inconvenience, the vestigial appendix of a less evolved state of being. Rather the body – or more precisely bodily experience – is the chief focus of the tectonic approach. Its relation to spatial form and material substance is encouraged by the application of various scalar operations that emphasize a close relationship between the individual and built space. These operations, be they the assignment of distinctive material properties to the horizontal and vertical surfaces of an interior or the specific detailing of a handrail or an entry canopy, give priority to the quality of the end-users' experience over the perspectival or graphical impact of a building's representation through visual media.

Contemporary tectonic architecture from the Pacific Rim is part of a long tradition of working closely with the substance of built form. The tectonic approach can be linked to many architectural and cultural traditions in the region – the Japanese fascination with detail and spatial clarity, the Mexican tradition of a rich, earth-bound architecture or the Australian preference for frugal assembly and constructional technique. Historically, an Asian-Pacific tectonic culture would include the works of architects as diverse as Tadao Ando, Glenn Murcutt, Fumihiko Maki, Luis Barragán, Pierre Koenig and Rudolf Schindler. Today many architects from the Pacific sphere continue to expand and reinterpret this tectonic tradition. Sendai-based architect Hitoshi Abe has created a remarkably experimental and wide-ranging body of projects that tests the limits of constructional practice. Daly, Genik temper the Los Angeles tradition for ad hoc materiality and expressive form with a tight and refined approach to the particular. In Sydney, Robert Dawson-Brown has cultivated a unique architectural approach that comfortably straddles the competing Modernist and Regionalist tendencies particular to current Australian architectural thinking. Singaporean architects KNTA have integrated an incisive knowledge of technical resolution with a distinctly South-east Asian spatial sensibility to produce a characteristic equatorial architecture. MORPHOSIS, recent converts to computerized design methods, continue to expand and refine their repertoire, producing convincingly insistent and resolved works in which composition, materiality, assembly and constructional technique are closely tied either to metaphoric or to direct alliances with the body. Kerstin Thompson's various small to medium-sized projects in Melbourne closely articulate detail and surface in order to draw discreet differentiations between interior and exterior, public and private. Working in the far reaches of the south-west Pacific, Christchurch architects Warren & Mahoney have designed a series of houses and public buildings that are taut reworkings of a limited but refined set of formal themes. Last, Seoul-born, US-domiciled architect Kyu Sung Woo has built a remarkable set of projects in Korea – judicious spatial delineations that impress with his close observance of material edge conditions and manipulation of surface openings and coverings.

The disparate projects presented in this chapter vary widely in scale, material application, constructional technique and formal concern. If these works depart from dissimilar starting points, they bring us collectively to a shared space, in which the body and the eye may appreciate the successful achievement of a corporeal architecture. What all the projects and architects have in common is an intensity of approach and resolution that reinforces an ontological experience of construction, a revealing of the *téchne* concealed in the tectonics of architecture.

Producers of space have always acted in accordance with a representation, the users passively experienced whatever was imposed on them.
Henri Lefebvre, *The Production of Space*

KYU SUNG WOO
CAMBRIDGE, USA

WHANKI MUSEUM

The Whanki Museum houses the collection of the contemporary Korean artist, Kim Whanki, in permanent and temporary exhibition spaces supported by a library, studio, café, shop, garden and assembly spaces.

Building a calm inner order

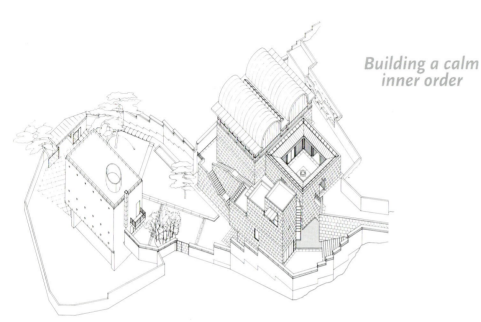

AERIAL PERSPECTIVE

OVER THE LAST ten years Kyu Sung Woo has designed a range of building types that respond to particular programmatic and site conditions found in Korea. These are works driven by a constantly evolving compositional approach, a keen awareness of material properties and characteristics and a sense of calmness. According to Hong Bin Kang, professor of urban planning at Seoul Municipal University, in Woo's architecture '…there are no dazzling visual effects or provocative configurations… Exaggeration, recklessness or high-handedness are absent from his work. Instead a quiet inner order is portrayed in his buildings, an order

WHANKI MUSEUM

The grouped buildings incorporate the aspects of nature that were important to the artist in his work: mountains, clouds, rocks and trees. The museum's layout connects it to its specific valley location and the Korean history of respect for the land.

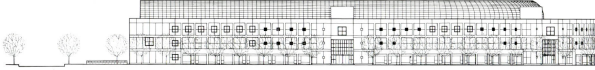

ATHLETES' AND REPORTERS' VILLAGE

The massing of the Olympic
Athletes' and Reporters' Village
recalls the introverted organization
of the traditional Korean village,
usually set into a bowl-shaped
terrain.

that seeps...calmly into the observer's mind.' Woo's design for
the 1988 Olympic Athletes' and Reporters' Village in Seoul was
planned to house 22,000 people during the Games and later
a community of 5,700 families. The massing of the Olympic
Athletes' and Reporters' Village recalls the introverted
organization of the traditional Korean village – an urban type
usually set into a bowl-shaped terrain with its houses set high
against surrounding hills and its public facilities concentrated
on lower elevations.

The Whanki Museum houses the collection of the
contemporary Korean artist Kim Whanki, in permanent and
temporary exhibition spaces supported by a library, studio, café,
shop, garden and assembly spaces. Woo considers buildings to
be physical and social entities, requiring spatial and social
reprieve and separation from the public sphere. The delineation

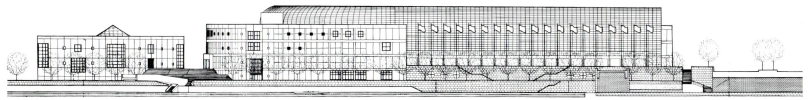

The villa, designed for an extended
Korean family, contains a traditional
courtyard and terraces that provide
views of the surrounding landscape.

of edge walls and the creation of centre provide this separation.
Windows, doors and stairs serve to moderate progression.
The elements of water and light establish centre. The building
incorporates the aspects of nature that were important to the
artist in his work: mountains, clouds, rocks and trees, and the
layout of the museum connects to its specific valley location and
the history of inhabiting the land. High ceilings in exhibit and
common spaces, combined with the limited area and complex
shape and steepness of the site, the scale of the valley and the
residential character of the neighbourhood, required limiting the
bulkiness of the massing. Therefore each programmatic element
is contained in a specific individual form, reflecting the Korean
method of additive site planning.

Woo's most recent building, Stone Cloud, represents a
new development in his approach to making appropriate
contemporary architecture. The villa, designed for an extended

STONE CLOUD

The villa is constructed of cast-in-
place concrete and finished with
stone veneer from a local quarry.
The window system features lead-
coated copper canopies, rolling
aluminium shutters and stainless-
steel extensions that meet flush
with the stone wall.

ELEVATION

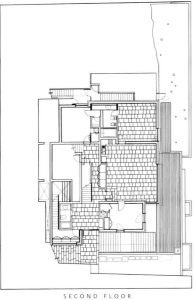

SECOND FLOOR

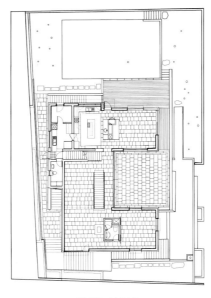

THIRD FLOOR

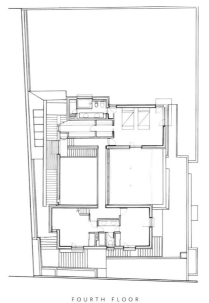

FOURTH FLOOR

Korean family, contains a traditional courtyard that provides views to the surrounding landscape. The primary living areas are situated around a central courtyard. The villa is constructed of cast-in-place concrete and finished with stone veneer from a local quarry. Interior finishes include stone flooring and plaster veneers, cherry veneer and stainless-steel panels. A fabric canopy over the courtyard looks festive and provides practical shade. Seoul, Woo's place of birth, is now a modern city with vast infrastructural systems that support millions of inhabitants, often without the benefit of proper planning processes. As he has written, '... it is a place devoid of modern design conventions. In this way, my architecture in Seoul has been, ironically, a search for the norm rather than individuality.'

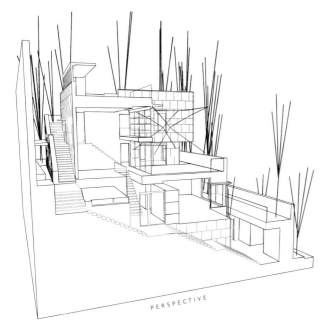

PERSPECTIVE

STONE CLOUD

Interior and exterior glass panels create transparency between spaces and a fabric canopy over the courtyard provides a festive environment for family celebrations and practical shading in the hot summer months.

DALY, GENIK
LOS ANGELES, USA

*Tempering expressive
form with a refined
approach to the particular*

MOOSER AVAKIAN RESIDENCE

The Mooser Avakian Residence involved the addition of a second storey to an existing 1948 bungalow situated on a typical 15 x 45-metre Santa Monica lot.

MOOSER AVAKIAN RESIDENCE

Daly, Genik positioned a simple sleeping loft over the older structure by removing the existing gable roof.

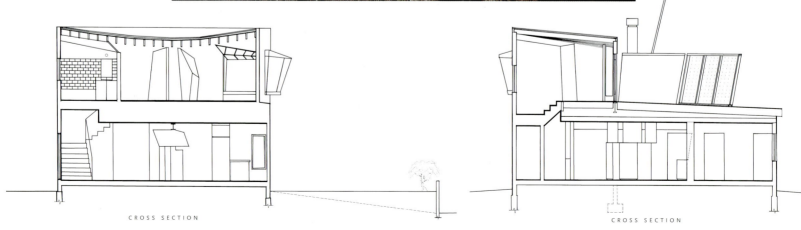

CROSS SECTION

CROSS SECTION

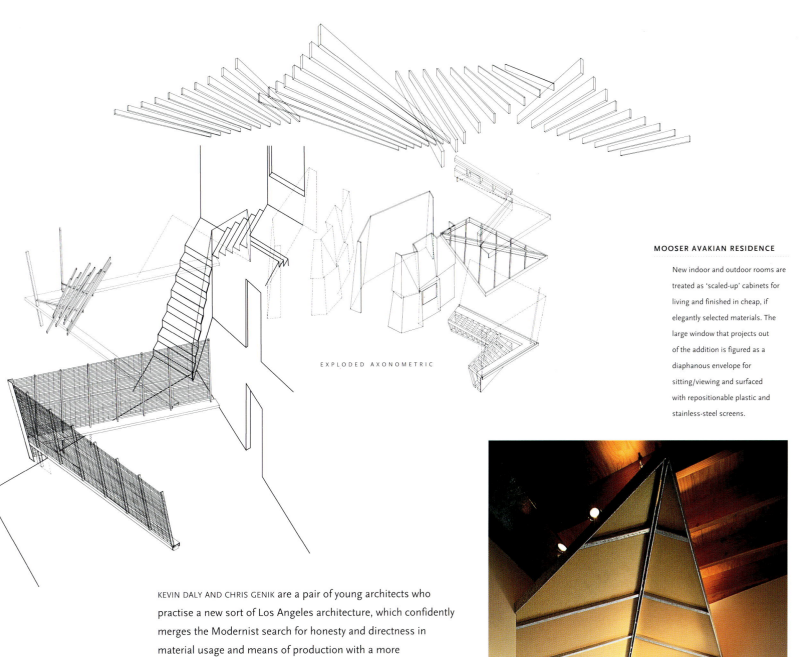

EXPLODED AXONOMETRIC

MOOSER AVAKIAN RESIDENCE

New indoor and outdoor rooms are treated as 'scaled-up' cabinets for living and finished in cheap, if elegantly selected materials. The large window that projects out of the addition is figured as a diaphanous envelope for sitting/viewing and surfaced with repositionable plastic and stainless-steel screens.

KEVIN DALY AND CHRIS GENIK are a pair of young architects who practise a new sort of Los Angeles architecture, which confidently merges the Modernist search for honesty and directness in material usage and means of production with a more contemporary tendency to see buildings as narrative structures or even theatrical mediums that favour the tactile surface over the pure plane and mannered fabrication over reductive structural design. For Daly and Genik, two designers who 'cut their teeth' working with Frank O. Gehry and Peter Waldeman respectively, the relationship of materials to the process of construction is an important and essential point of departure for their architecture. Daly, Genik's projects for residences and small institutional facilities reflect their continuing research into the field of material properties and the interface between the conventions of standard construction and the possibilities of customized fabrication.

The Mooser Avakian Residence involved the addition of a second storey to an existing 1948 bungalow situated on a typical

15 x 45-metre Santa Monica lot. Daly, Genik positioned a simple sleeping loft over the older structure by removing the existing gable roof. The old lower storey and the new upper storey were joined by a steel moment frame that braces the old structure and bears the load of the new construction. New indoor and outdoor rooms are treated as 'scaled-up' cabinets for living and finished in materials chosen for both their cheapness and elegance. The large window that projects out of the addition is figured as a diaphanous envelope for sitting/viewing and surfaced with repositionable plastic and stainless-steel screens. Steel-trowelled plaster, bar grating, medium-density fibreboard and exposed roof framing complete this simple but visually compelling project.

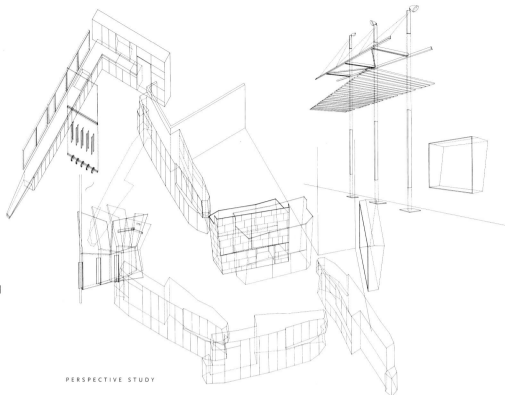

PERSPECTIVE STUDY

TARZANA RESIDENCE

This renovation of a large 1960s suburban tract house employs a simple but refined palate of materials to create a surprisingly light-filled and unusual dwelling in an otherwise nondescript neighbourhood.

The residence's original fireplace (LEFT) was built out and clad in ribbed and rolled aluminium by the Daly, Genik to create a new central focal point within the house. Discreetly placed apertures (RIGHT) create sneak views in and out of this jewelled box of geometries.

The Tarzana Residence, Daly, Genik's renovation of a large 1960s suburban tract house, employs a series of controlled spatial moves and a simple but refined palate of materials to create a unique, surprisingly light-filled dwelling in an otherwise nondescript neighbourhood. Initially, Daly, Genik opened up the formerly cramped interior by lifting the roofline and removing six internal walls to create one large loftlike space. In turn, this singular space was redefined by a series of freestanding and movable components – a pivoting spruce screen, finely assembled Douglas fir cabinets and freestanding furniture pieces designed by the architects. These elements swirl around the residence's original fireplace, reconfigured by Daly, Genik to create a new central focal point within the house. Built out and clad in ribbed and rolled aluminium, the fireplace gathers and reflects light like a jewelled basilisk. Polished cabinets of fir, ash and bird's-eye maple, smooth kitchen counters of glass and green granite and partitions of sandblasted glass add atmospheric inflections to this residential conversion.

Daly, Genik combine the Los Angeles architectural bias for relaxed construction and emphatic form with a taut and polished approach to the distinctive qualities of materials and means of assembly. 'We have always been interested in the artists of the everyday, in interpreting how things are made,' says Kevin Daly, '[but] our architecture is about detailing a simple material into something that is extremely high-performance.'

TARZANA RESIDENCE

Polished cabinets of fir, ash and bird's-eye maple add warmth to the living areas.

KERSTIN THOMPSON
MELBOURNE, AUSTRALIA

Reconceptualizing the corporeal pleasures of architecture

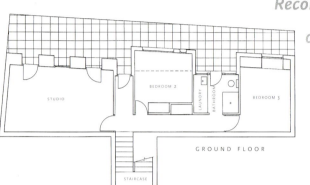

GROUND FLOOR

MORGAN HOUSE

Located in Lorne in the state of Victoria, the house is embedded in a hill that faces the awesome Southern Ocean.

MORGAN HOUSE

Like a massive retaining wall, the Morgan House hold backs the earth at its rear, giving a strong presence to the protected courtyard there.

KERSTIN THOMPSON heads a young practice that has established itself as a significant and innovative reference point in contemporary Australian architecture. Her work is marked by its consequential material presence and a consistent interweaving of landscape and architecture, mass and detail, interior and exterior.

The Morgan House, Thompson's earliest commission, uses massive form to capture space. Located in Lorne in the state of Victoria, the house is embedded in a hill that faces the awesome Southern Ocean. Like a massive retaining wall, the Morgan House holds back the earth at its rear, giving a strong presence to the protected courtyard there. Here Thompson explores a strong division between light and dark space. Airy 'day pavilions' are perched over a heavy 'night podium'. Composed viewlines flow into the building's masonry mass and out towards the ocean through a series of carefully composed openings. The Webb Street residence, Thomson's most recent project, involved the extension and conversion of an existing house into a studio and residence. Connections between living and working rooms, eating and sleeping areas and circulation or observation spaces are interlocked by a compositional strategy that skilfully knits new and old into a playful dance of material and connective possibilities.

Thompson's practice celebrates movement – the orchestration of the body's journey between spaces, light levels and terrain conditions. By interlocking material and spatial connections to produce interstitial conditions between building and street, structure and landscape, surface and detail, Thompson has created buildings that seek to exceptionalize the body as the primary subject of architecture. As Thompson has noted, her projects celebrate both form and detail 'as useful ways of conceptualizing some of the corporeal pleasures of architecture; because, so often, it is literally only through touching detailed forms … that bodies become linked to architecture'.

MORGAN HOUSE

Composed viewlines flow into the building's masonry mass and out towards the ocean through a series of carefully composed openings.

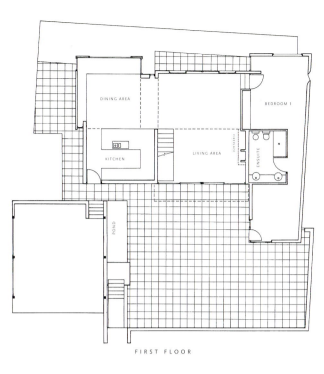

FIRST FLOOR

CLEMENGER/BBDO OFFICES

This computer-generated montage dextrously depicts Thompson's proposal for the Melbourne offices of Clemenger/BBDO. Using a refined range of materials and finishes, the design weaves reception, production and office spaces into a seamless environment.

KNTA
SINGAPORE/LONDON, UK

CHECK'S HOUSE

The house is composed from a wide and rich palette of materials.

Building an expressive architecture immersed in the cultures of East and West

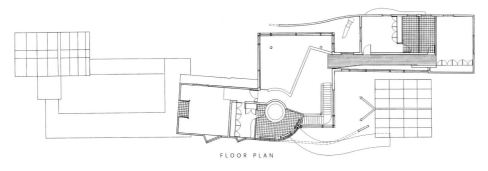

FLOOR PLAN

KNTA was formed in London in 1990 and opened another studio in Singapore three years later. Their work reflects an immersion in the cultures of East and West and it is through this synthesis that they hope to create buildings that bridge the idiosyncratic frameworks of each region.

Check's House is emblematic of their approach to developing a confident Singaporean architecture that merges indigenous material traditions, practices and forms with

CHECK'S HOUSE

Like many traditional Singaporean houses, this project is set east-west and lengthwise on an elongated lot. It is entered from the side via a gradually sloping timber ramp connected to a suspended glass carport and pedestrian canopy.

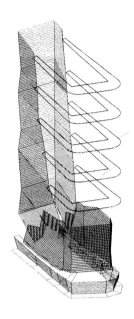

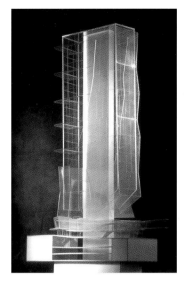

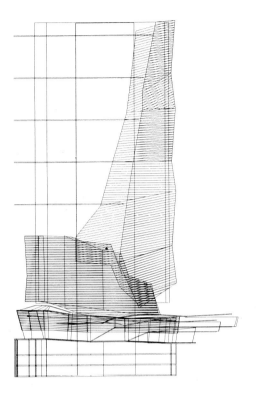

MAYBANK CHAMBERS TOWER COMPETITION ENTRY

This competition entry for a banking hall projects a dynamic image of currency exchange through its use of light-reactive screens and sculptural glass forms.

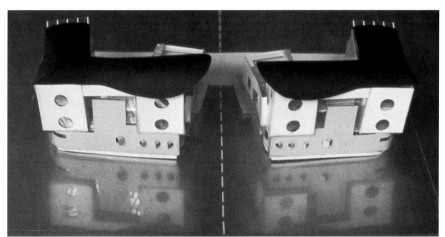

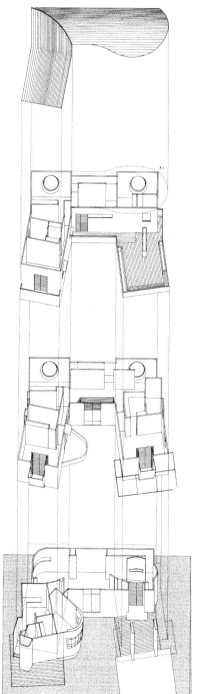

innovative engineering and building technologies. In the manner of many traditional Singaporean houses, this project is set east-west and lengthwise on an elongated lot. It is entered from the side via a gradually sloping timber ramp connected to a suspended glass carport and pedestrian canopy. The driveway is in line with the main body of the house. Two separate wings extend out of this central mass, a box-shaped volume that contains the living and family areas. Following the tradition of many Asian houses, entry into the house is delayed. The living area enjoys views of the public botanical gardens adjacent to the house but traditional tropical-timber shutters can provide privacy.

SHUDE HOUSING

These two houses are symmetrical, mirrored structures inspired by the Chinese appreciation of symmetry and oriented using Chinese geomancy. The duplicated roofs, covered in metallic sheets or slate tiles, are reminiscent of the twin carps often reproduced on rural Chinese New Year's woodcut prints or on traditional kites – a motif of double happiness.

EXPLODED AXONOMETRIC

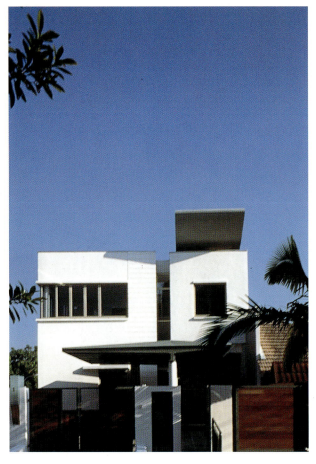

1 CORFE PLACE

A curved external plate (OPPOSITE) recalls a ship's naval architecture.

1 CORFE PLACE

Entry is marked by a split in the house's face (ABOVE). Sculptural interior volumes (RIGHT) are toplit by the bright tropical sun.

ELEVATION

The house's main enclosures are constructed in reinforced concrete and this basic framework provides points of attachment for cladding elements and suspended shading features. The flat concrete roof is protected from Singapore's blazing equatorial sun by a secondary roof made of matte anodized aluminium panels attached to the house by steel trusses bolted on to raised concrete plinths. This secondary roof creates a cooling air space, testing a traditional idea for tropical roof structures in new material form.

Shunde, a city in the Guangzhou region of southern China, was the setting for two houses fronting a lake. These mirrored structures were inspired by the Chinese appreciation of symmetry and oriented using Chinese geomancy. The duplicated roofs, covered in metallic sheets or slate tiles, are reminiscent of the twin carps often reproduced on rural Chinese New Year's woodcut prints or on traditional kites – a motif of double happiness. KNTA create tectonically rich buildings, which unite a sharp knowledge of technical resolution with a distinctly Asian spatial sensibility.

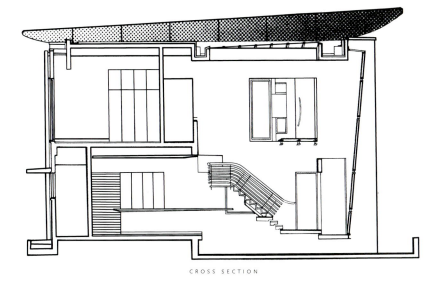

CROSS SECTION

ARCHITECTURE WARREN & MAHONEY
CHRISTCHURCH, NEW ZEALAND

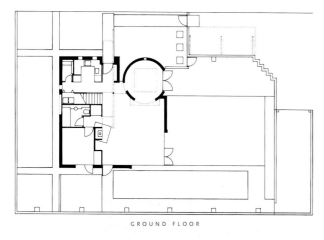

GROUND FLOOR

Creating a dynamic new formal tradition in the South Pacific

HOUSE CARR

A simple cube with geometric openings and the brightly coloured tower reflect the client's work as an artist and creator.

HOUSE CARR

This project involved the design of a two-storey residential home in Fendalton, a suburb of Christchurch.

ARCHITECTURE WARREN & MAHONEY is one of New Zealand's most established and respected offices. The practice was begun in the mid-1950s by Sir Miles Warren and Maurice Mahoney in Christchurch, but today it operates out of four separate offices in Auckland, Wellington, Christchurch and Queenstown. The projects shown here are by one of the Christchurch directors, South African-born architect Thom Craig. Craig's work for Architecture Warren & Mahoney has reinvigorated Christchuch architecture and brought attention to the firm from as far away as Milan and Tokyo.

Christchurch was laid out in a stylized, uniform colonial grid on an alluvial plain, interrupted only by the Avon River, which meanders across the city. Into this rather charming city Craig has placed a series of formally sophisticated buildings. His designs for residences, a church, a railway station, a regional airport and a convention centre have sidestepped the current penchant in Christchurch for faux-pitched-roof historicism and have evoked a strong public response. But if his works seem at times indifferent to Christchurch's cultural conservatism, Craig has argued that they are clearly affected by a local tradition of making and craftsmanship, earthquake considerations, and indigenous or Pacific influences.

The O'Connell House, Craig's striking design for a clifftop residence in Christchurch, demonstrates his dedication to developing a formalized architecture, which is at once both highly personal and of its place. Consisting of two distinct volumes combined to form an idiosyncratic form, the house is balanced firmly on the top of a volcanic cliff facing the Pacific. On the topmost edge of the site a two-level, charcoal masonry box rises up to meet the road boundary. Alongside this massive box, a two-level, eye-shaped, corrugated-steel drum is perched on thin poles, causing the drum to appear to be floating, tethered to its more substantial neighbour only by a lightweight steel-and-

CHRISTCHURCH RAILWAY STATION

On a site next to a historic water-tower, the railway station is a steel-framed waiting hall sandwiched between two stainless-steel boxes.

glass gantry. In the split between the two volumes an axial extension defines areas of entry and transition and draws the external fabrics of galvanized steel and charcoal plaster into the house. The Christchurch Railway Station, designed concurrently with the O'Connell House, extends some of the formal signatures found in the residence into a considerably larger public programme. On a site next to a historic water-tower, the railway station is a steel-framed waiting hall sandwiched between two stainless-steel boxes, which contain offices, storerooms and restrooms. Covered by an elegant, curved and floating roof, the station is connected both visually and physically to the 22-metre-high water-tower by a curving garden wall, which encloses the arrival and departure garden courts.

As an immigrant, Craig has had to modify his attitudes radically to absorb the social, regional and physical particularities of the New Zealand environment. In reconciling the formal vocabulary he developed as an architect working in Johannesburg with his newly adopted South Pacific home, Craig turned not to local architectural traditions first but to New

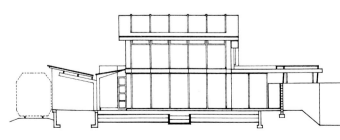

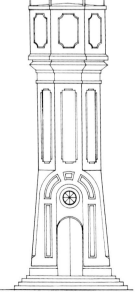

ELEVATION

O'CONNELL HOUSE

This residence on the east coast of New Zealand's South Island is carefully balanced on the top of a volcanic cliff overlooking the South Pacific. The house is composed of a two-level charcoal masonry box positioned next to a two-level, eye-shaped, corrugated-steel drum. The split between the two volumes defines areas of entry and transition and draws the external fabrics of galvanized steel and charcoal plaster into the house.

O'CONNELL HOUSE

The corrugated-steel skin on the drum is peeled back to command views of Christchurch's Pegasus Bay, Sumner Bay and Brighton Spit to the south (LEFT). The drum, dramatically perched on thin poles, appears to be floating (OPPOSITE).

Zealand's contemporary artists, finding great inspiration in the work of Colin McCahon and Stephen Bambury. By acknowledging and questioning these influences Craig has said that he hopes to contribute to the emerging crosscultural dialogue in New Zealand.

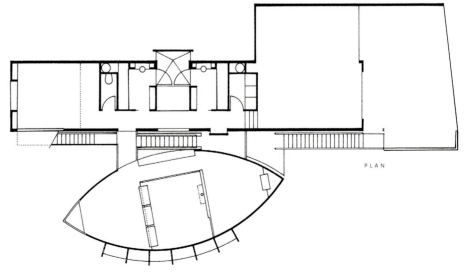

PLAN

DAWSON-BROWN ARCHITECTURE
SYDNEY, AUSTRALIA

PADDINGTON TOWNHOUSE

Access to the new sub-level was created by the addition of a staircase within glass and timber-louvred wood structure attached to the rear façade and set into the stone-faced courtyard.

Creating a dynamic new formal tradition in the South Pacific

SECTION

PADDINGTON TOWNHOUSE

This project involved an addition to an 1850s townhouse. The design called for the excavation of a new sub-basement and courtyard area in order to create kitchen, dining and living areas.

ROBERT DAWSON-BROWN is an emerging Sydney architect whose compelling residential designs effortlessly straddle the opposed Regionalist and Modernist leanings current in Australian architectural debate. He effectively argues that his perspective grows out of his preference for '… unpretentious poetic functionalism, using natural tactile materials and expressed structure … overlain with the need to create joy for both the experience of architecture and the making of it.'

Dawson-Brown's recent addition to a townhouse in Paddington, ten minutes' drive from Sydney's heart, involved the restoration of the ground floor and first floor of the 1850s terrace house and the excavation of a new sub-basement and courtyard area in order to create kitchen, dining and living areas. Access to the new sub-level was created by the addition of a staircase within a tightly resolved glass and timber-louvred wood structure attached to the rear façade and set into the stone-faced courtyard. The Brigadoon House in Perth, Australia, was the winning design in a competition sponsored by a building-materials company.

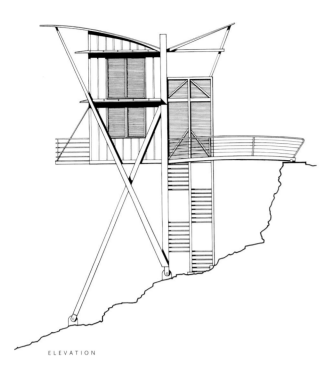

ELEVATION

This design reflects a 1920s beach cottage and adds new accommodation, a pool, terraces and a tree-house studio. The tree house is accessed via a bridge over the pool. The materials, forms and planning are all designed to reinforce the natural context.

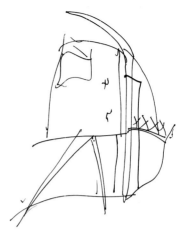

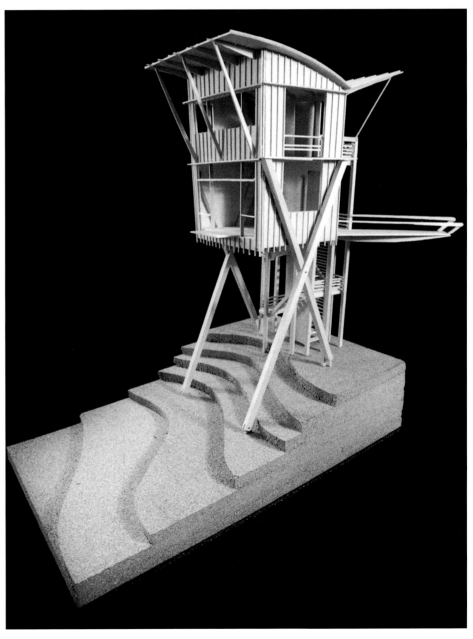

Briefed to produce an environmentally conscious building that could respond to the hot, dry and windy microclimate of its site, the architect employed both passive and active environmental design solutions. The house is carefully laid out along the site's east-west contours within a natural clearing between a valley-like grassland and a steep, rocky slope. The structure is a load-bearing steel portal frame clad with external skins that vary materially according to climatic orientation. To the south a rammed-earth thermal wall protects the house from winter winds and summer bushfires. Glass louvres and doors maximize northern winter sun and the eastern and western elevations are predominantly weatherboard-enclosed bedrooms, which cool quickly on summer evenings.

The Bellevue Hill Residence, an early project completed by Dawson-Brown in collaboration with designer Caroline Casey and architect Kimberly Ackert, is set on a narrow sloping block with spectacular views of Sydney's magnificent harbour and its city centre. This topographical situation inspired the development of the house as two stacked pavilions placed parallel to the slope and orientated to the views. A pier structure ties the house to bedrock five metres beneath a subsurface of sand. These piers internally frame the views and provide a separation between spaces in the open plan. A three-metre-high stone fin wall directs entry into the house through a sliding door that gives way to a double-height entry space. The open-plan kitchen is in the centre of the ground level and provides easy access to the family room, dining room and a formal living area. Bedrooms are on the upper level, for privacy. The basement level accommodates car parking,

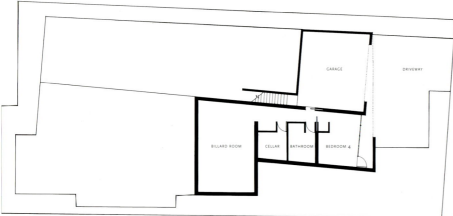

a guest bedroom, a cellar and a billiard room. Large overhangs to the west blend a brise-soleil and automatic sun-blinds to protect the interior from the afternoon heat and scooped roofs between the concrete piers introduce eastern light into the bedrooms and encourage natural air movement throughout the house.

Architecture for Dawson-Brown is emphatically 'realist' without pretence to theory. His process of design struggles to absorb and translate into the building the *genius loci* of each site by means of the layering of material and constructional expression.

BASEMENT

BELLEVUE HILL RESIDENCE

The Bellevue Hill Residence (OPPOSITE) is set on a narrow sloping block with spectacular views of Sydney's magnificent harbour and its city centre.

BELLEVUE HILL RESIDENCE

The site's topographical situation inspired the development of the house as two stacked pavilions placed parallel to the slope and orientated to the views.

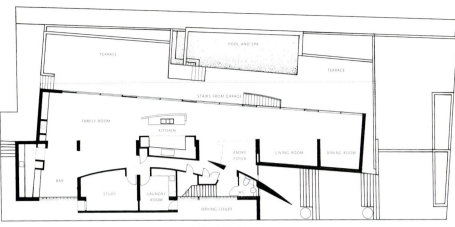

GROUND LEVEL

MORPHOSIS
LOS ANGELES, USA

ASE DESIGN CENTRE

ASE Taipei involved the introduction
of a design centre into a mixed-
use housing and retail complex in
Hsichih – a fast-growing suburb
on the outskirts of Taipei.

*Creating a dynamic
architecture closely allied
with the body and its scale*

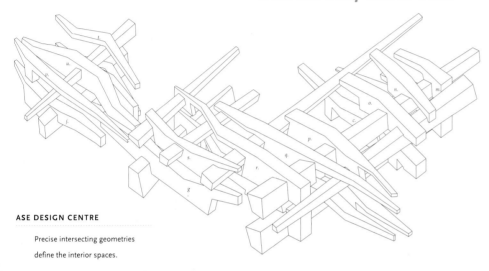

ASE DESIGN CENTRE

Precise intersecting geometries
define the interior spaces.

MORPHOSIS ARE FRONT-RUNNERS in the international design community and leaders within the Los Angeles school of architecture. Their first commissions for small houses and restaurants in southern California were ground-breaking designs that pushed out the boundaries of composition and invention. Today, with an international portfolio of large projects in Asia and Europe, Morphosis continue to augment and cultivate their architectural approach and formal techniques, producing deeply resolved works in which composition, materiality, assembly and constructional technique are closely allied, metaphorically or directly, with the body and its scale.

ASE Taipei involved the introduction of a design centre into a mixed-use housing and retail complex in Hsichih, a fast-growing suburb on the outskirts of Taipei. Two formal languages or systems, eggs and shards, were employed by the architects to help make sense of the space. The eggs, made of rusty steel plates, extend and mimic a rounded swelling at the western end of the complex. Morphosis repeat this curved form three times throughout the complex, stacking it to contain the eating, exhibition and lecture areas. The shards are a series of kinked, white-plaster blade-walls that follow the variable lines of the structural column grid, encasing the building's metre-square concrete columns in deep walls that often rise seven metres off the ground floor. These shards fly across the complex on east-west 'flight patterns' but are punctured by openings that allow for north-south perpendicular movement. A floating school of fishlike, fibreglass sculptural pods or seeds swims parallel to the blade-walls, completing the composition and adding a wry touch to the fecund, egglike spaces.

The Blades Residence explores the relationship between landscape and the signification of domestic iconography. The house takes the form of a curved roof plane sheathed in bonderized metal and nestling closely into the landscape. In the

ASE DESIGN CENTRE

Two formal languages or systems,
eggs and shards, define internal
spaces and synthesize the design
centre's requirements into distinct
zones. The shards are a series of
kinked, white-plaster blade-walls
that follow the variable lines of
the structural column grid, encasing
the building's metre-square
concrete columns in deep walls
that often rise seven metres off
the ground floor.

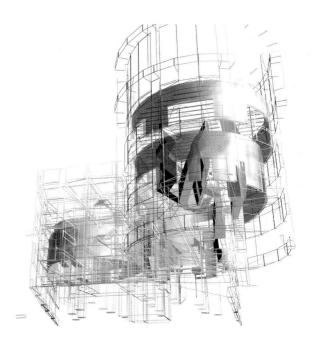

ASE DESIGN CENTRE

The shards (ABOVE) fly across the
complex on east-west 'flight patterns'
but are punctured by openings that
allow for north-south perpendicular
movement to run against the grain
of the shard arrangement. The eggs
(BELOW), made of rusty steel plates,
extend and mimic a rounded swelling
at the western end of the complex.
Morphosis repeat this curved form
three times throughout the complex,
stacking it to contain the eating,
exhibition and lecture areas.

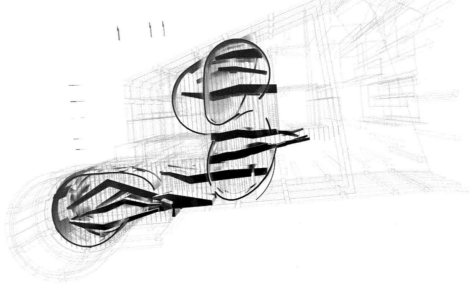

interior, three main spaces are laid adjacent to five smaller
exterior rooms. The house forms intersects with an arcuating
concrete garden wall that creates a sixth large exterior room.
Instead of merely planting objects directly over the ground,
Morphosis transcend the traditional opposition between figure
and ground or between passive site and active building, beyond
the Corbusian model of machine and nature as a dialectic.

The Sun Tower is Morphosis's first completed project in
Korea. The ten-storey tower, in a district to the west of Seoul's city
centre, bridges two very constricted urban sites, which demanded
a generic programme and a maximized zoning envelope. The
project is composed of two slender concrete-framed towers
which are united by a sliver of vertical public space that runs up
the building. These volumes are punctuated by a highly regulated
fenestration pattern and wrapped in a folded, origami-like cloak
of perforated-steel mesh frames clipped to the building's concrete

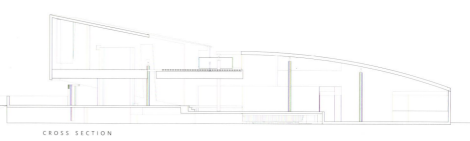

CROSS SECTION

BLADES

The house's form intersects with an arcuating concrete garden wall that helps make the site into an architectural element.

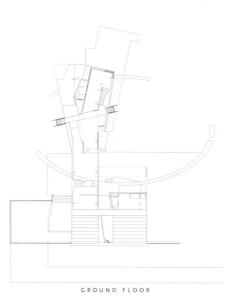

GROUND FLOOR

frames. The tower's steel skins glimmer in the sun and create optical effects that make the edifice seemingly dissolve into its urban setting, its surfaces undergoing continuous transformations and shifts in opacity.

Morphosis have moved away from the highly organized Platonic systems of invention and complicated constructional assemblies that defined their early works. But if their newer works are more plastic and volumetric, Morphosis have clearly not abandoned the intensity and resolution that have defined canonical projects such as the Crawford Residence or the Cedars-Sinai Comprehensive Cancer Center. Indeed, as Thom Mayne, principal of Morphosis, has said, '… [if our] earlier projects had always been motivated by the need to regain a certain sense of authenticity, an identity or stability of place … the current work is less concerned with recovering what might have been lost than with new opportunities … emerging organizational possibilities enabled by new technologies. The sense of loss with regard to the craft and the material properties which have been so fundamental to our architecture is mitigated by an optimism about these new possibilities.'

BLADES

The house explores the relationship between landscape, architecture and domestic iconography.

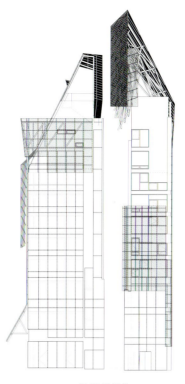

ELEVATION

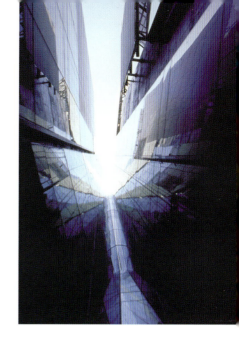

SUN TOWER

The project is composed of two slender concrete-framed towers which are united by a sliver of vertical public space that runs up the building.

SUN TOWER

The ten-storey tower, in a district to the west of Seoul's city centre, bridges two very constricted urban sites that demanded a generic programme and a maximized zoning envelope.

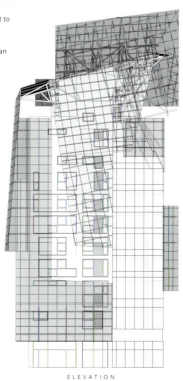

ELEVATION

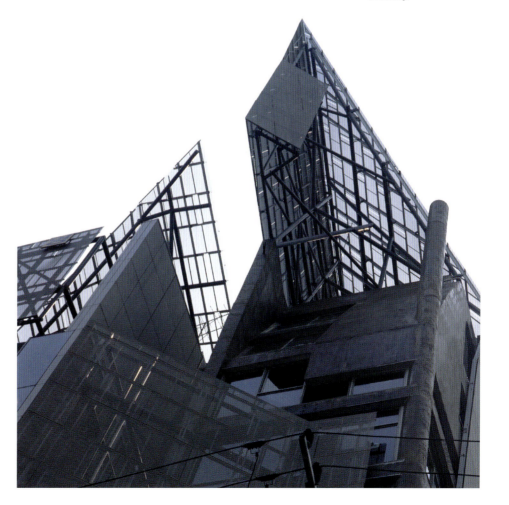

ATELIER HITOSHI ABE
SENDAI, JAPAN

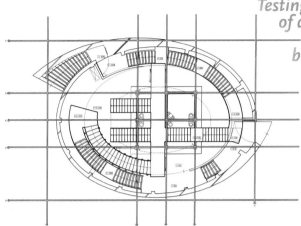

PLAN

Testing the limits of contemporary constructional practice by radical experimentation with form

MIYAGI WATER-TOWER

A public infrastructure project, the Miyagi Water-Tower is designed to hold up to 150 tonnes of water at a height of 27 metres.

MIYAGI WATER-TOWER

The tower's expressive internal steel work recalls the Russian Contructivist aesthetic.

HITOSHI ABE believes that architecture is a kind of reflective medium; a spatial and material transfer of human will into reality. Neither the direct user nor the direct constructor of the environment, the architect must operate in between life-use and physical production. The architect, then, exists only in the process of making space and so architecture is alive only in the process of its making. For Abe, based in the city of Sendai in Japan's Miyagi Prefecture, '… architecture is … like clay recording the movement of the fingers of both hands; one hand is the human's will and the other is the condition of the environment. Architecture is the record of the conversation between those subjects, it is the medium to reunite them.'

Abe's C House project began as a game of codes and spatial moves played across its site – a field formed by building regulations and topographical conditions. Two playing pieces were invented to allow play – one a white vertical ribbon of continuous wall, the other a black horizontal bar. The white piece is characterized by concepts of non-flammability, enclosure, high insulation, privacy and a Western style of spatial arrangement. The black piece is characterized by concepts of flammability, openness, low insulation, publicness, continuity and a Japanese style of spatial arrangement. The Miyagi Stadium, a project designed for use by up to 50,000 spectators, is an attempt on Abe's part to loosen up the concept of the stadium, which he argues has not changed since the Roman Age. Abe reverses the usual bowl-like stadium type to become a hill and then puts the two types – bowl and hill – together to create an unstable swirl of half-enclosed, half-open public space. The Shirasagi Bridge project involved the wrapping of an existing bridge in a new structure in order radically to alter its appearance. Seventy-four steel right-angled triangles form the new composition. Each triangle is rotated, expanded or contracted in a fluid series of movements in order to define a new skin surface for the bridge while also

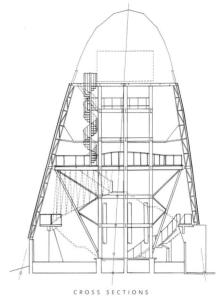

MIYAGI WATER-TOWER

Abe rejected a solid, singular form so that the tower could fuse with its environment. To achieve this end, the tower's potential mass was weakened into a structural lattice-work defined by lines of force – a structural striptease. Ivy will eventually creep up the construction, creating what Abe calls a sort of architectural negligée.

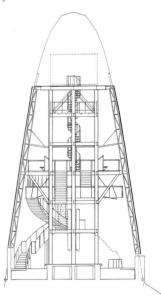

accommodating lighting, railing, weight and clearance demands and limitations. Another public infrastructure project, the Miyagi Water-Tower, is designed to hold up to 150 tonnes of water at a height of twenty-seven metres. Although basic requirements for vertical and horizontal strength and a large base suggest a uniform, blocklike structure, a solid, singular form was rejected so that the tower could fuse with its environment. To achieve this end, the tower's potential mass was weakened into a structural latticework defined by lines of force – a structural striptease. Ivy

SHIRASAGI BRIDGE

The Shirasagi Bridge project involved the wrapping of an existing bridge in a new structure in order radically to alter its appearance.

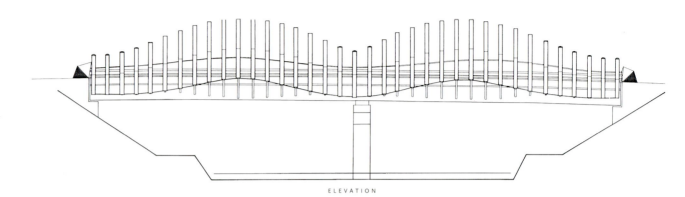

ELEVATION

SHIRASAGI BRIDGE

Seventy-four steel right-triangles form the new composition. Each triangle is rotated, expanded or contracted through a fluid series of movements.

CROSS SECTION

will eventually creep up the construction, creating what Abe calls a sort of architectural negligée. Abe's latest project, the A House, was designed for use by a two-generation family. Borrowing ideas for this house from his xx-Box temporary exhibition system, an earlier project, Abe has created a structural assemblage that frees the plan by using an A-framing system (structural frames that look like a series of 'A's) made out of reinforced concrete. Two sets of thick walls provide lateral support and a series of vaults act as both roof and floor surfaces, allowing for long, free-span, columnless spaces within the house.

SHIRASAGI BRIDGE

The steel right-triangles define a new skin surface for the bridge while also accommodating lighting, railing, weight and clearance demands and limitations.

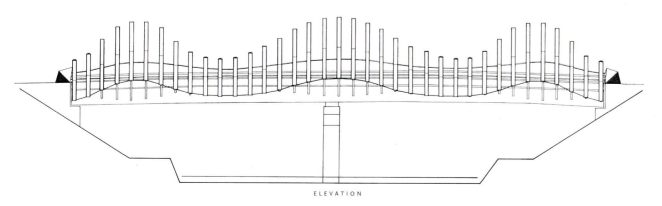

ELEVATION

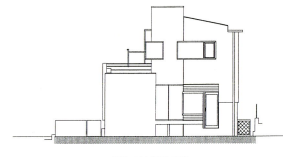

END ELEVATIONS

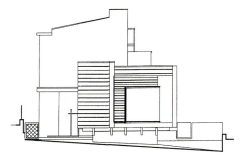

C HOUSE

The C House is composed of two competing spatial typologies: one a closed vertical Western-style volume; the other a black horizontal Japanese open frame. The interior merges modern structural means with the Japanese tradition for spatial fluidity.

ELEVATION

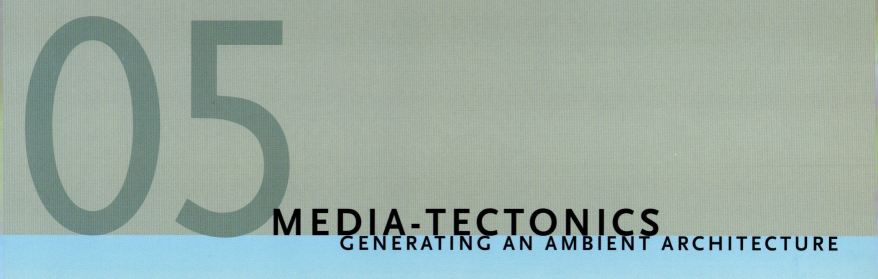

05 MEDIA-TECTONICS
GENERATING AN AMBIENT ARCHITECTURE

The highly publicized ascent of the cultural and geographic construction known as the Pacific Rim is often credited to the technological advancements of the information age. Japan is a paradigmatic example of a nation repeatedly depicted as having been resuscitated in the post-war period thanks to the modernizing technologies of the assembly line and the microchip. In recent popular discourse the

Consider the word rim: A rim unites – it unites across oceans, across ethnic and racial divides. It presumes a unity … A rim is a horizon: the horizon of capital, of history, of space and time. It is a topology for the 'suppression of distance' said to be characteristic of our times.
Christopher Connery, *Pacific Rim Discourse: the US Global Imaginary in the Late Cold War Years*

physical and financial development of the Pacific Rim has been regularly coupled with the rise of the various virtual and real mechanisms that constitute the still-developing transnational computer network called the Internet. Indeed, the Rim – perhaps more than any other global region – is a space almost overdefined by the presence of contemporary technology, be it in reality or in Hollywood's various imaginary filmic visions of the area (*Bladerunner, Black Rain*, etc.). Certainly, if one considers the vast weblike tangle of undersea telephone cables that link Asia, Oceania and the Americas, the innumerable communications satellites that float over the Pacific or the technology-rich regions of Silicon Valley or greater Tokyo, the predominant image that emerges of the Pacific Rim is of a superconnected global region, a collection of nations on the forefront of technological innovation. Whether or not this is entirely true, the contemporary cultural and social economies of the Rim have quickly developed in no small part because of the speed and efficiency of contemporary electromagnetic transmission. Significantly, this new means of communication has allowed human interaction to occur outside the normative constrictions of real time and geography and thus suggests a second Pacific Rim – a despatialized and seamless virtual geography of rapid informational interchange and rearranged 'natural' temporal sequence. In this new context, the importance of location as an indicator of true proximity along the Rim has been erased and replaced by online time and telepresence. Online time is universal

Urbanism is in decline, architecture in constant movement, while dwellings have become no more than anamorphoses of thresholds. In spite of people nostalgic about History, Rome is no longer in Rome, architecture is no longer in architecture, but in geometry; the space time of vectors, the aesthetic of construction is dissimulated in the special effects of the communication machines, engines of transfer and transmission; the arts continue to disappear in the intense illumination of projection and diffusion.
Paul Virilio, *The Aesthetics of Disappearance*

time and to be online all the time is to be everywhere at once and nowhere in particular. This is an ambient, multidimensional space in which the fluid informational soft architectures of the new media flow over the hard architectures of the contemporary city, creating an indeterminate environment, an interface between the public and the private, the local and the global, the real and the virtual. This is the technology-saturated, informational and symbolic world that some architects around the globe now claim as a new and novel context for architectural exploration and experimentation.

Architects in the Asia Pacific region are dynamically exploring the technologized territories of this new horizon by way of both built form and unbuilt ideas for physical, informational or hybridized spaces. On one hand, some architects such as Kei'ichi Irie are actually working within the Internet itself, creating three-dimensional interfaces for the as-yet undefined social, cultural and economic virtual cities of the future; a new digital urbanity that will act as an interface between the virtual and the real. On the other hand, such designers as the Anglo-French-Malaysian team dECOi–Objectile and the Los Angeles-based architect Neil M. Denari are working directly with advanced space-modelling softwares and computer-aided manufacturing technologies to create sharply attuned buildings for a future in which architecture may become more akin to the precise fields of numerically generated industrial design and manufacturing. Meanwhile, Foreign Office Architects and GAS are generating buildings, which, while no less technologically advanced, are more specifically about mapping out, tracking and responding to the new social orders and relationships that have developed in the crosscultural, globalized world. Finally, Toyo Ito has cultivated a highly synthetic architecture that seems to weld together many of these concerns into highly determinate 'nomadic' objects, which float effortlessly in the indeterminate fields of the contemporary Japanese metropolis. Taken together, the various projects presented here represent an architecture that can confidently drift through the existing city or alongside the symbolic flows of new social transaction without losing itself in the flood of signals that defines our age. This is truly an ambient architecture; an environmental intimation of the new millennium's urban and architectural possibilities.

The architectural projects presented here should serve to dissuade us from the outcome Wentinck predicts for us because they suggest a future that involves existing not in the vacuum of electronic transmission or

It looks as if two bio-technic types will survive: the static type, that makes his home his world, and the dynamic type, that makes the world his home. By means of digital highways ... and comprehensive data-transmission systems, the world can be reduced to the dimensions of a static dwelling ... living will be synonymous with being enclosed in a cocoon surrounded by a flowing electronic world ... the dynamic type will run around in the real world in what's left of archaic nature.
Victor Wentinck, *Interactive Interstates 1*

on the cultural margins of an archaic reality, but in a space that combines the richest qualities of the virtual and the real worlds. These projects help to reconstitute an interface between the body, architecture and technology within the space of information exchange and production. By working with new technologies and weaving digital technology into the body of architecture itself, these architects are beginning the long, hard task of inventing new sorts of living conditions and spatial relationships. Surprisingly, their work returns architecture to some of the most basic factors of human existence – the very issues that enframe architectural production itself: habitation, the nature of human activity and communication and exactly how our new work, leisure and living conditions may help determine the outlines of our cities. Just as the expanse of Modern Space – figured so clearly in Mies van der Rohe's horizon-projected architecture – served so well to demonstrate humanity's engagement with the world through the technologies of the industrial age, this expansive post-industrial architecture, a new sort of spacemaking, powerfully demonstrates our embodiment in the world through the technologies of the digital age. Rather than uncritically ride the gravitational pull taking us all towards the new digital horizon, these architects propose an architecture that confronts the dynamic and reactive informational landscape.

dECOi—OBJECTILE
PARIS, FRANCE / KUALA LUMPUR, MALASIA

Exploring new spatial possibilities and novel modes of invention/ production offered by cutting-edge technologies

ECO-TAAL

Detail view of entrance with parking canopy eliminated.

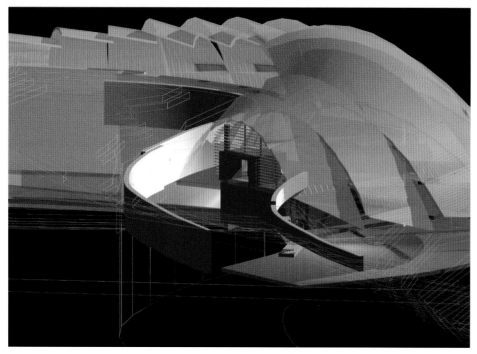

dECOi is a new type of architectural practice dedicated to exploring the spatial possibilities and novel modes of invention/production that are offered by rapid technical change. Established in Paris in 1991 as a loose, research-based architectural group focused initially on competitions, theorization, experimental installations and teaching, dECOi has evolved into a 'nomadic' practice, split between studios in Kuala Lumpur and Paris and supported by state-of-the-art technology. Led by Mark Goulthorpe, dECOi remains fundamentally flexible and loose in order to afford and sustain collaborative and beneficial mergers with engineers and theorists in both Europe and Asia. Most recently dECOi has formed a partnership with the industrial design group Objectile, another collective led by French technologist, theorist and designer Bernard Cache.

ECO-Taal is a recent project for an ecological centre located some 160 kilometres south of Manila on the slopes of the magnificent Taal caldera-volcano, one of the world's lowest volcanos and one of several still active volcanos in the Philippines. The ECO-Taal compound is embedded in the slope of a hill that faces out towards the caldera – a vast circular crater some thirty kilometres across, filled with water and punctuated at its centre by the cone of the volcano itself. Conceived as a sequence of stepped levels that follow the site's contours, the

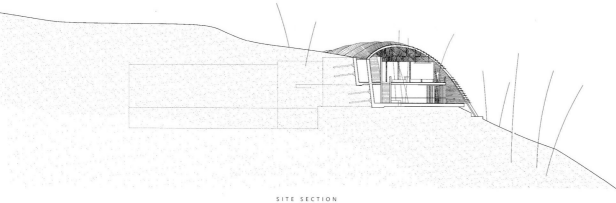

SITE SECTION

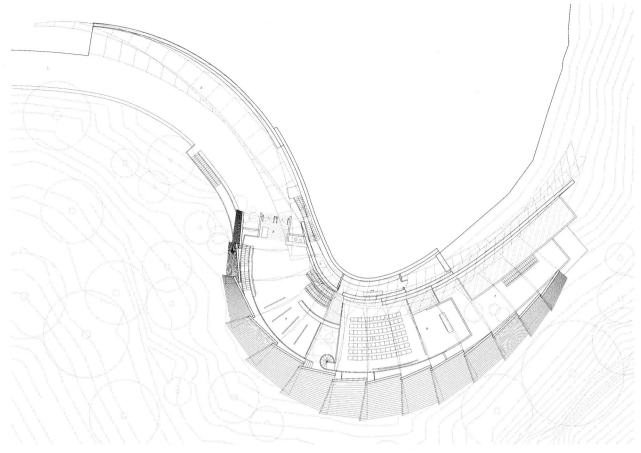

UPPER ENTRANCE LEVEL

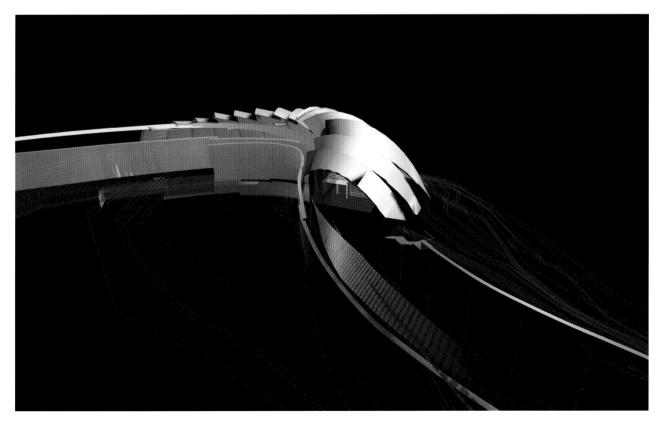

ECO-TAAL

View of the structure's back
from the hillside above.

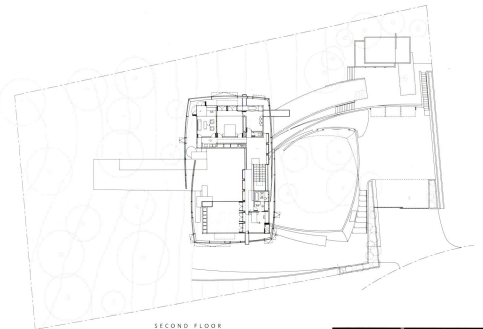

SECOND FLOOR

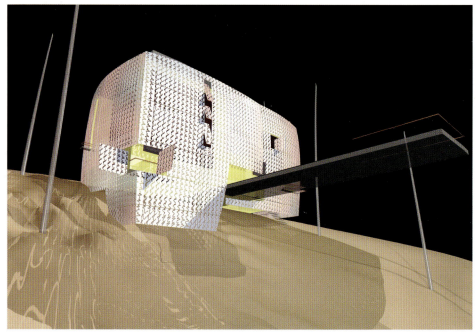

ecological centre is wrapped in a series of organic and curvilinear
'carapace' shells, which disguise the terraced platforms and
re-create the forms of the terrain. The sustainable-timber,
sculptural outer skin is described by the architects as a leaf-frond
gently draped over the hill, peeled into several twisting segments,
which permit solar penetration from the east, protect from the
sun's harsh western glare and admit prevailing sea breezes
from south and west.

The Pallas House, a commission for a contemporary tropical
house, was designed from the developer-client's brief for a
building that attains the formal sophistication of product design
and presses the limits of available manufacturing, construction
and form-generation technology. Formally the house is articulated
as two simple gestures: the first is what dECOi refer to as a 'heavy

negative' – an excavation that models the entrance court out of
the project's steep terrain; the second is a 'light positive'
composition that builds the house itself out of a grouping of
fragile boxes wrapped in a delicately curving and perforated,
numerically generated steel shroud. The enveloping shroud is
formulated as seven complex-curved metallic shells, each
distinct but mathematically coherent, on to which will be
mapped a constantly shifting, numerically generated perforation,
an electronic hieroglyphic developed by Objectile to give an
optical movement – a 'shoal of fish' flicker to the house. This

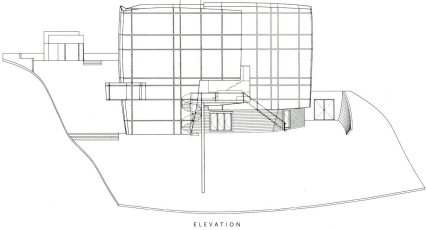

ELEVATION

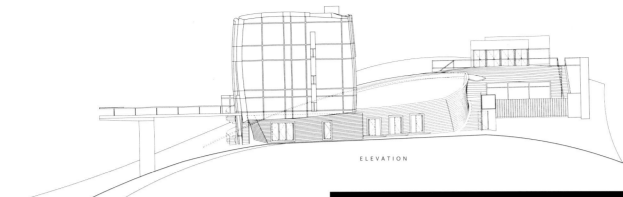

ELEVATION

environmental carapace, a lightweight and reflective breathing skin of minimal surface-to-volume ratio and minimal mass, acts like a climatic filter, using the logics of contemporary cladding systems to overcome the tropical heat and solar gain. The Pallas House, dECOi emphasize, is not a simply graphic exercise, but closely follows research and production already carried out by Objectile in their coordination of complex-curve generative software with numeric command machining from computer models. The design of the house highlights a shift in the base logics of production in that it requires complex one-off components to be produced precisely and relatively cheaply, and the manufacture of a series of similar objects, mathematically coherent, but each different in its form.

PALLAS HOUSE

The elements of the house behind the skin (ABOVE). The exterior view shows the transparency of the house at night (LEFT).

FOREIGN OFFICE ARCHITECTS
LONDON, UK

PUSAN HIGH-SPEED
RAILWAY COMPLEX

Seen from above, the Railway
Complex reads as a series of
undulating strips or ribbons
in a landscape.

*Tracking and responding
to the new social orders
and relationships in
the globalized world
with a generative
architecture*

PUSAN HIGH-SPEED
RAILWAY COMPLEX

FOA's competition entry for a High-
Speed Railway Complex pays special
attention to the organization of
social space through the use of a
plastic formal language.

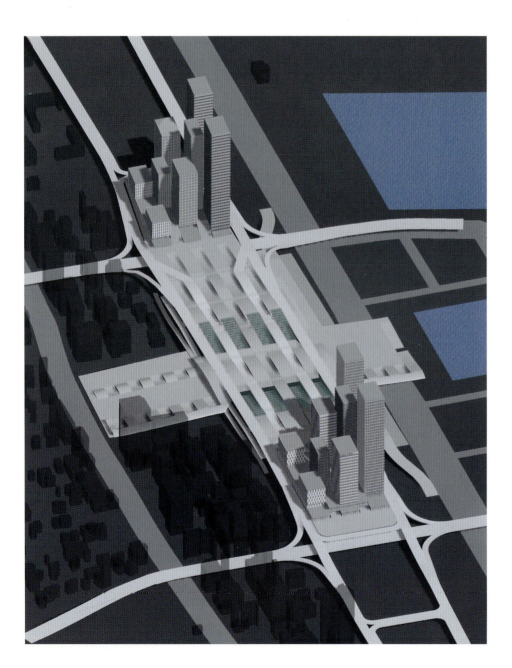

FOA PARTNERS Farshid Moussavi and Alejandro Zaera-Polo are two
architects who see the strange oscillations between the global
and the local not just as a reflection of the troubled crosscultural
conditions endemic in the late capitalist culture of our age but also
as a field of opportunity for spatial exploration. For FOA this
situation invites architectural consideration and it must be
critically embraced as an area for creative experimentation. FOA
have developed a generative process and formal approach to
architecture which is similar to systems theory – one in which
the manipulation, often by digital means, of certain forms of
abstracted information can provide a useful way for the architect
to escape from the deformations of the global or the conventions
of the local without sacrificing the specific. By analyzing use
patterns, population distributions, topographies and topologies,
FOA organize abstract forms into architectural ideas that can be
manifested in a spatially convincing but abstract fashion. FOA
operate with the idea that material realities and not signs or codes
are the best vehicle for the construction of ideas in the globalized
world. Rather than embody ideas through textual reference, they
pursue a material practice that confronts the lack of cultural
consensus stemming directly from the oversaturation of the world
by informational technologies. If their early designs for various
cultural institutions admirably illustrated this approach, their
much-publicized competition-winning entry for the Yokohama
International Ferry Terminal forcibly demonstrated the potentially
extraordinary physical manifestations that such a deliberately
methodological approach may grant.

   FOA beat a field of 650 competitors to win the international
competition for the ferry terminal by ditching preconceived
notions of what such a terminal should look like. Instead they
concentrated on informationally and spatially specific issues –
flows of public circulation, interaction levels between travellers and
citizens and the relationship between the pier and its urban

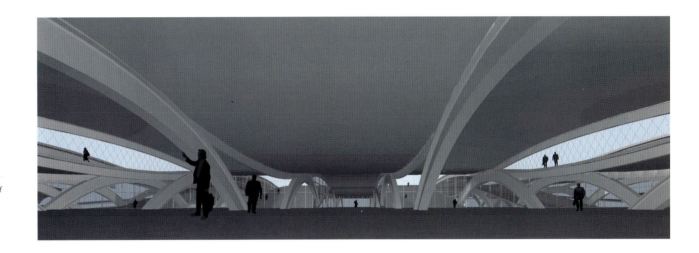

setting. Their research led them to develop a pier which will be part-park, part-transport-interchange hub. Their project links an undulating roof plane of sequenced green or open spaces with the groundline of the city itself, creating an urban garden in the sea. Passengers and visitors will be able to enter the complex from the roof surface through a number of openings which open into a bifurcating series of flexible internal zones and event spaces. FOA suggest that this work represents the primary theme of the competition brief – a folding of the city into the ocean. They argue that the project's elements deterritorialize each, by a process of spatial mixing and collapse in which ground folds to become structure and then folds again to become a new ground.

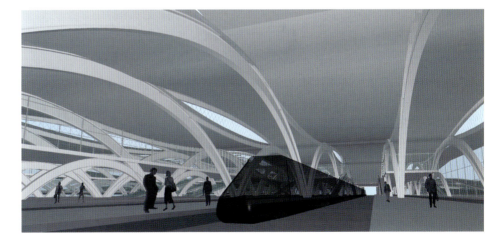

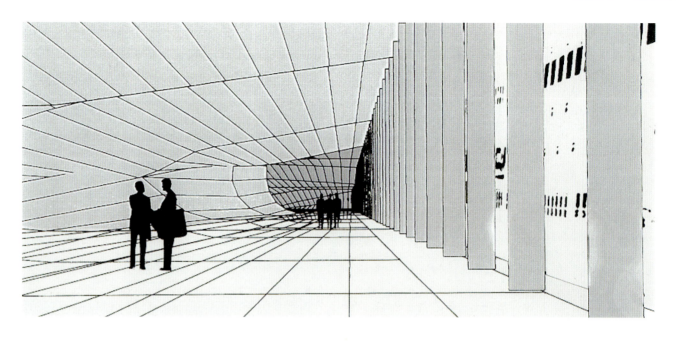

YOKOHAMA INTERNATIONAL FERRY TERMINAL

FOA beat a field of 650 competitors to win the international competition for the Yokohama International Ferry Terminal by ditching preconceived notions of what such a terminal should look like. The long section shows the flowing public concourse as an almost organic entity. Boarding (RIGHT) and waiting (BELOW) lounges are contained in spaces which are marked by a blurring of envelope and structure, floor and column and ground and floor.

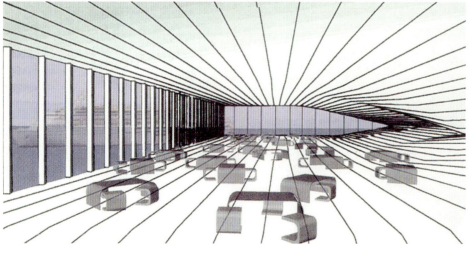

According to FOA, this reduction of distinctions between envelope and structure, floor and column and ground and floor '… blurs the typological definitions of functional elements in a terminal through a forced continuous space; the functional resolution of the programme operating as device of estrangement of the urban ground, leading to an a-typological public space.'

FOA's project for the Meyong Dong Cathedral for the Korean Catholic Church pursues themes and working methodologies similar to those applied to the Yokohama International Ferry Terminal, but in a more dense and urban setting. Annexed to a Cistercian brick complex built in the nineteenth century by French missionaries, the site for the project is surrounded by an elevated highway and the most important shopping street in Seoul. Here,

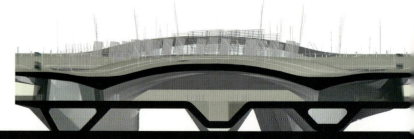

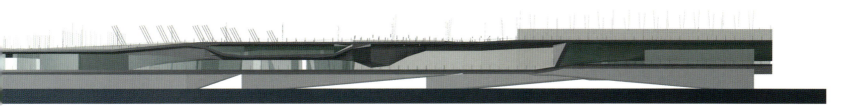

YOKOHAMA INTERNATIONAL FERRY TERMINAL

Shops drift within the terminal's flowing circulation spaces (LEFT). The undulating roof plane of sequenced green or open spaces connects the terminal with the groundline of the city itself, creating an urban garden in the sea.

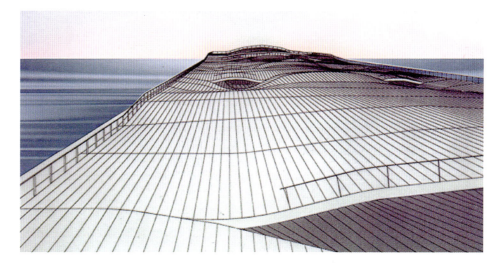

YOKOHAMA INTERNATIONAL FERRY TERMINAL

Sectional studies show the process of spatial mixing and collapse in which ground folds to become structure and then folds again to become a new ground.

KANSAI SCIENCE CITY LIBRARY

This competition entry for a public
library in a new development
near Osaka called Kansai Science
City is defined by a series of parallel
folded roof plates that hover on a
thin column grid.

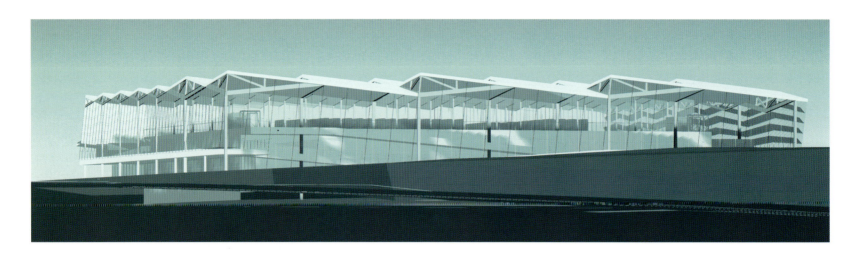

KANSAI SCIENCE CITY LIBRARY

Gentle ramps lead users through
the interior (LEFT). Gaps between the
roof strips (BELOW) bathe the interior
in continuous light.

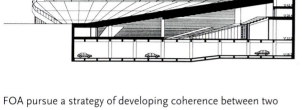

FOA pursue a strategy of developing coherence between two conflicting environments by making a bowl from the urban landscape in order to accommodate fixed auditoria, meeting rooms and shops enclosed within a covered stadium. Instead of exploiting the fragmentation and difference suggested by the site, FOA offer a unity of sorts – a topological manipulation of surfaces that allows for a continuity of space – an urban unity at Seoul's geographical centre.

MEYONG DONG CATHEDRAL COMPLEX, SEOUL

FOA's project for the Meyong Dong Cathedral for the Korean Catholic Church pursues a strategy of developing coherence between two conflicting environments by making a bowl from the urban landscape in order to accommodate a brief for fixed auditoria, meeting rooms and shops enclosed within a covered stadium.

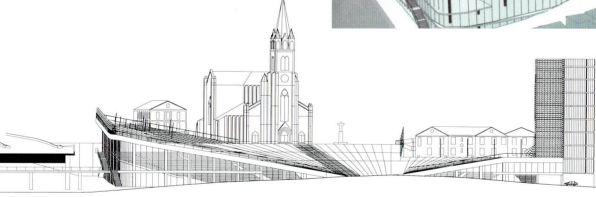

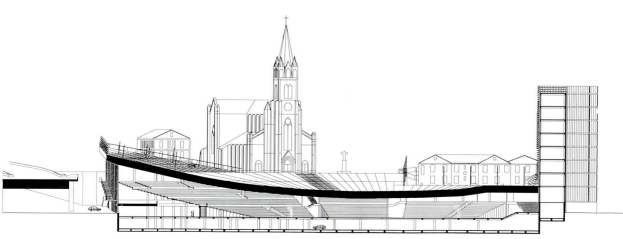

GAS
LONDON, UK / KUALA LUMPUR, MALAYSIA

*Exploring extraordinary
and complex morphological,
programmatic and
climatic variables with
new technological means*

KUALA LUMPUR SUBCENTRE

The KLSC project is an urban-scaled, mixed-use master plan for an eighty-hectare urban subcentre in Kuala Lumpur's outskirts.

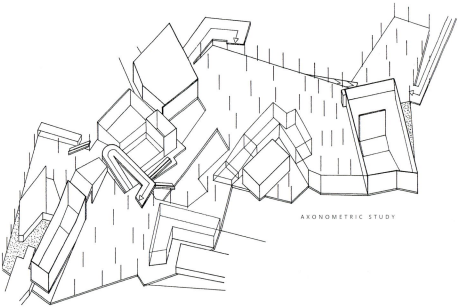

AXONOMETRIC STUDY

GAS is a young, five-member architectural practice that exists in part because of the advent of electronic networks and communication systems, which have closed the gaps between far-off places and distinct temporal zones. GAS is literally split between Europe and Asia, its creative base being in London and its operations in Malaysia. This allows GAS to be in action twenty-four hours a day, concepts and projects oscillating between two time zones via the networks of electronic exchange. London is treated as a laboratory of ideas in which architectural, technical and urban research provides both a theoretical launching pad and an incubation period for concepts, which are later tested on real projects and at varying scales and/or speeds in South-east Asia. GAS is developing an infrastructural approach to architecture,

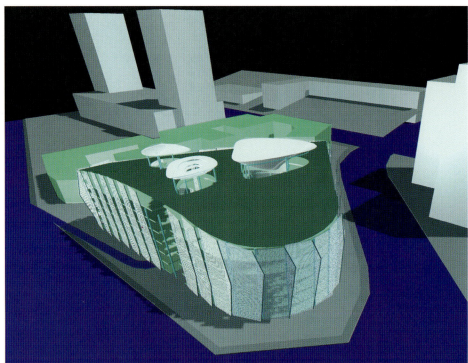

K OFFICE

The K Office corporate headquarters project in Subang, Malaysia, involved the design of a transport company's new headquarters.

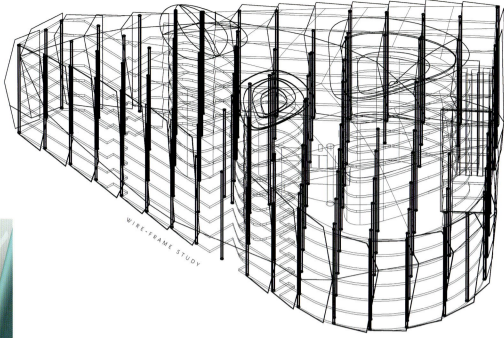

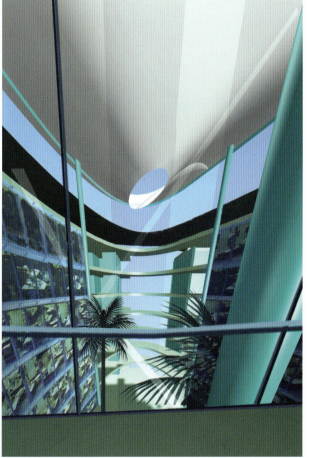

landscape and the urban condition. Employing advanced software engineering at both the conceptual and production stages of design, GAS has discovered that mediated and artificial procedures yield extraordinary and complex morphological, programmatic and climatically sustainable results.

The KLSC project by GAS is an urban-scaled, mixed-use master plan for an eighty-hectare urban subcentre in Kuala Lumpur's outskirts. It is being developed over ten years in two phases. The *tabula rasa* site will eventually serve 250,000 people – reflecting how Kuala Lumpur is shifting from a monocentric city to a dispersed polycentric urban structure. In response to this, GAS has employed a process of sophisticated three-dimensional mixing – a type of urban sampling – to build up urban diversity quickly. Four non-exclusive city types were sampled for their organizational and programmatic qualities, then topologically projected on to the site and finally adjusted to local planning constraints. The result is a planning arrangement in which overlapping programmatic elements interlock and fuse

K OFFICE

Three large canopied atriums bring exterior space into the building. Each of the canopied voids reflects a different environmental theme – air, land or water. The project is wrapped in a continuous wave pattern.

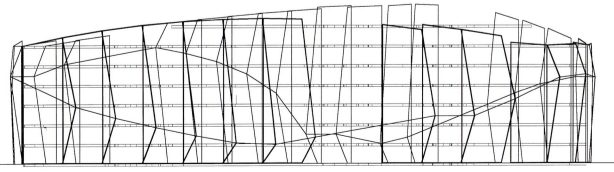

WIRE-FRAME STUDY

C2 EATING

C2 Eating is a blurring of food and media, using both as materials for consumption. The enclosure includes spaces for cooking, serving, seating and art exhibits.

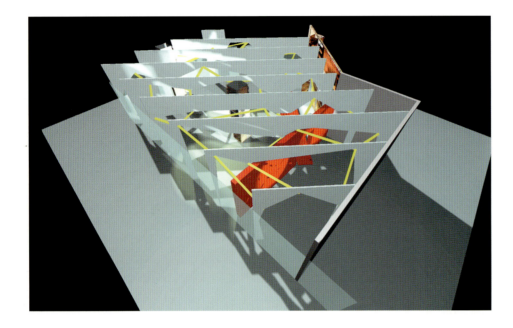

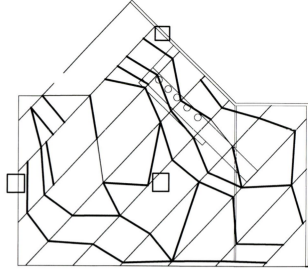

PLAN

both plan and section, creating blurred generic urban categories and shaping social spaces that promise to create a vital and layered environment. The K Office corporate headquarters project in Subang, Malaysia, involved the design of a transport company's new headquarters. Situated at a busy traffic intersection, the building was to include offices, conferencing facilities, a daycare centre, prayer rooms, exhibition spaces and a cafeteria, all to be stacked into a single volume. GAS proposed a strategy of

C2 EATING

GAS proposes that food be consumed as media (dried food sample sections, projected images of food and videos of preparation processes). Spaces are programmed for eating at different speeds. Animated surfaces enhance the eating experience, to be both gastronomic and visual.

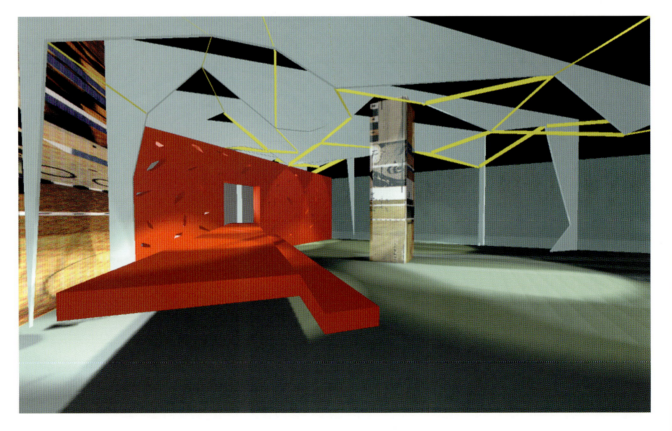

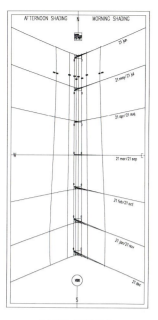

CROSS SECTION

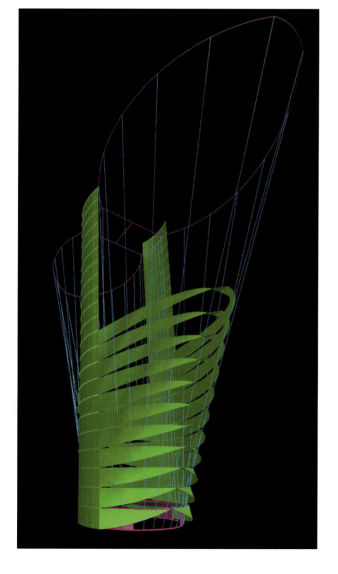

WIRE-FRAME STUDY

OPTIMAL FORM

This project was made possible by writing a computer program that aimed to emulate the way in which nature optimizes its use of material and energy. An initial cylindrical form was 'grown' in response to the Malaysian sun. Surfaces were given the potential to develop and move under the influence of the mathematics of solar geometry and the constraints of the Malaysian environment. The shape deformed outwards towards the directions of greatest solar radiation so as to optimize its self-shading form. Green planar bands then developed in response to undesirable levels of radiation still penetrating the inner core of the building form.

reversing this inside-outside relationship by internalizing the building's exterior space within three large canopied atriums. Each of the canopied voids would reflect a different environmental theme – air, land or water – literally the transport company's three main modes of carriage. Wrapped in a semi-transparent skin of screened glazing, the exterior panels were to form a continuous wave pattern that was meant to reflect the client's twenty-four-hour-a-day, non-stop operations.

GAS works in a new zone of urban activity that seems to predominate in the new world – the new paradigm of collapsed scale, mixed use and multiplied opportunity. Projects vary from small-scale interiors to large-scale urban plans but are forced to become adaptive and flexible, whatever the scale, because of the demands of the marketplace. The boundaries between scales, timelines, spatial limitations, programmes and cultures are often blurred. GAS argues that these conditions create new freedoms, allowing architects to produce intensified spaces with multiple characteristics. There is a positive acceptance of these facts and trends in Asia that makes GAS optimistic.

NEIL M. DENARI / COR-TEX
LOS ANGELES, USA

*From machine architectures
to digitally generated
smooth spaces, a West
Coast visionary emerges*

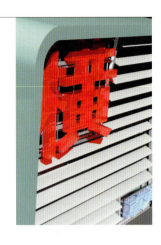

TOKYO HIRISE

This thirty-metre-high building
provides eight repetitive floors
of highly minimized one-room
apartments in a dense Tokyo
setting.

TOKYO HIRISE

The structure is set in a densely
built-up part of Tokyo.

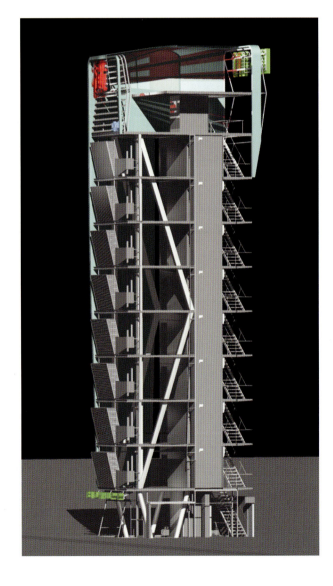

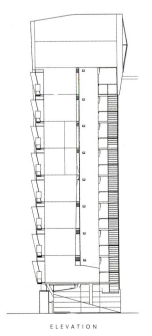

ELEVATION

DURING THE mid- to late 1980s Texas-born, Los Angeles-based
architect Neil M. Denari attracted a wide following for himself
among architecture students, other architects and critics despite
the fact that he had no major built works to his name. Denari's
reputation at the time rested solely on his formidable drawing
skills and a handful of competition entries (notably his Tokyo
Forum proposal of 1990 and his Westcoast Gateway project of
1988), which had established him early in his career as a
significant architectural visionary.

Denari's numerous 'unbuilt' proposals from the 1980s for
libraries, houses and even a monastery obsessively reiterated a
machine aesthetic or a mechanistic inflection and explored the
physical and philosophical possibilities of a 'machined
architecture'. These barely Utopian, technologically driven visions
and his obvious lack of interest in a performative or straight
functionalist architecture made the work difficult to classify as
either late Modern or even High-Tech. The eminent architectural
historian and critic Kenneth Frampton has observed that Denari's
projects inhabit '… a modern world which, in the last resort, has
to be seen as the domain of anxiety and pain'. Indeed, Denari's
view of technology is hardly optimistic in the usual sense of the
word and his thinking about architecture is closer to the
sensibilities of writers such as Ballard or Burroughs than it
is to the shiny, optimistic dreams of science fiction.

More recently, the machine aspects of his work have further
dissolved into his interests in the fuzzier aspects of contemporary
culture and digital technology. His latest works, such as the
Vertical Smooth House, Interrupted Projections project at Gallery
MA or his entry for the Kansai Science City library competition,
utilize smooth, seamless geometries to connect disparate spaces
and direct user flow. His newer projects have taken on an almost
soft, pregnant or even blobby quality as the hard edges that
defined his earlier hand-drawn proposals have given way to

GALLERY MA

GALLERY MA

The Interrupted Projections project was built in 1996 in a Tokyo art and architecture space called Gallery MA.

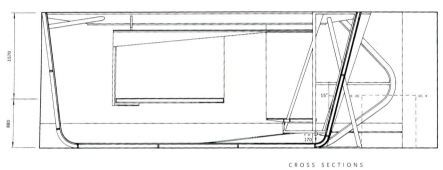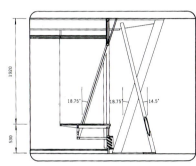

CROSS SECTIONS

GALLERY MA

Denari created what he has suggested is an abstract, architectural conception of the space of global communication and information exchange. The space is a continuously bending smooth surface that has logos and symbols floating over its green surface.

ELEVATION

ELEVATION

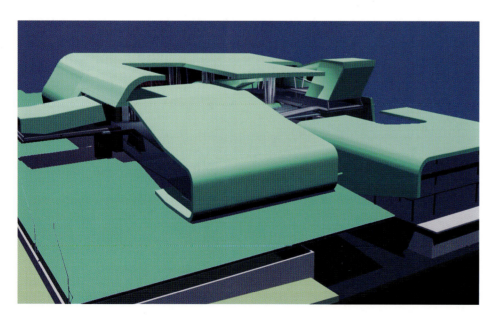

seductive, fluid techno-scapes produced on high-end workstations. For the Interrupted Projections project in 1996, in a Tokyo art and architecture space called Gallery MA, Denari created what he has suggested is an abstract, architectural conception of the space of global communication and information exchange. Noting that the historical origin of such a space might be the cartographer's rolled map, Denari developed a concept he coined the Worldsheet – an inherently bendable surface for the inscription of information and/or symbols. The space he built uses a continuously bending smooth surface that has logos and symbols floating over its green surface. Its greenness is in itself a kind of artificial or supernatural colouring, a fashionable code for nature today. In a way, the work is essentially about interpreting such cultural codings. However, this small gallery in Tokyo also reflects how the geometric possibilities made available to the

The library's internal volumes are made up of consistent, smooth, seamless geometries — spatial diagrams that connect disparate spaces and direct user flow and information exchange.

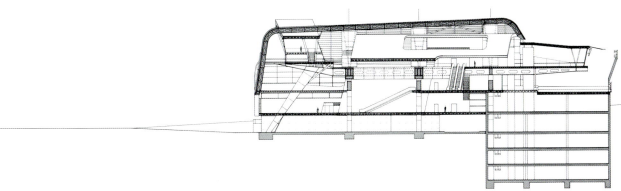

CROSS SECTION

KANSAI SCIENCE CITY LIBRARY

Treelike column clusters sprout from the apex intersection at structural moments in the building.

architect by the computer can benefit unique new spatial configurations and assemblies.

What these refined, yet elastic spaces demonstrate, beyond a semantically driven use of reference, is that Denari's architecture now describes the smooth flows of the information world on an urban scale. But, perhaps more importantly, his built projects clearly reveal that Denari is no longer just an architectural visionary — he is an architect and a builder of consequence.

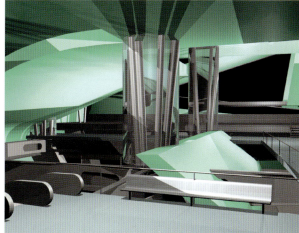

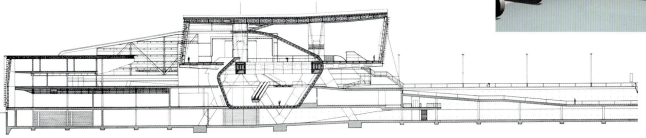

CROSS SECTION

MASSEY RESIDENCE

This house for a young graphic designer is located on a typical 15 x 45-metre Los Angeles lot, the typical and basic North American suburban subdivision.

ELEVATION

MASSEY RESIDENCE

Front and rear elevations follow the basic extruded form of the overall volume.

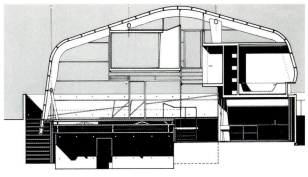

CROSS SECTION

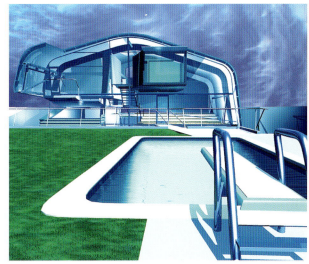

MASSEY RESIDENCE

Internal space revolves around a staircase that connects seven different levels (ABOVE). This 3-D sectional study of the Massey Residence (BELOW) reveals its complex floor stacking.

MASSEY RESIDENCE

A sectional study (TOP) reveals the shifting nature of the house's internal volumes and its place in an excavated cut in the land. The backyard (ABOVE) is a luminescent green field punctuated by the chlorine artificiality of a small lap pool.

KEI'ICHI IRIE / POWER UNIT STUDIO
TOKYO, JAPAN

Moving beyond the narrow dialectic of virtual versus real into a new space defined by the fusing of these conditions

TOKYO CONTINUUM

Exhibited at the 1996 Venice Biennale of Architecture, the Tokyo Continuum project is an ongoing research proposition that explores the visual representation of potential 'information scapes' within the built environment.

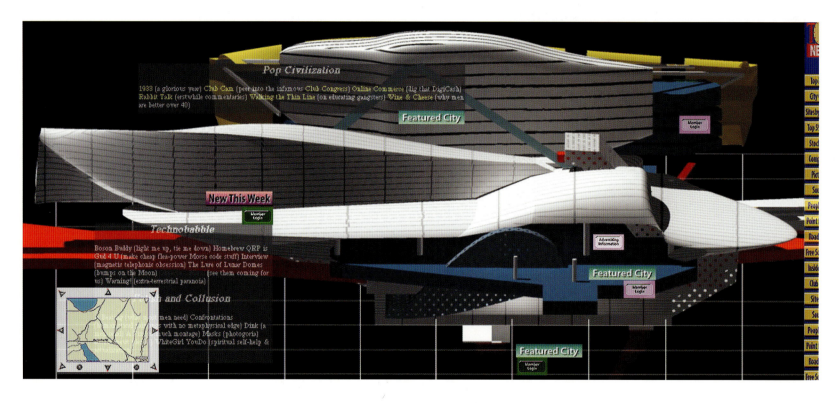

Kei'ichi Irie is building a new sort of architectural space within the Internet itself, creating three-dimensional intermeshes and interfaces for the indefinable social, cultural and economic relationships that will soon spread across the chasm between the virtual and the real. His Tokyo Continuum, shown here, is a project that sharply brings into focus how architectural methodologies and metaphors can create new syntaxes of space, form and activity within the informational worlds created by electronic interchange.

The Tokyo Continuum project is an ongoing research proposition that explores the visual representation of potential 'information scapes'. Fundamentally, this is a database project, a collaborative work, which Irie has developed with Andreas

Shneidor. 'Information scapes' are conceived as new database/interface environments that represent locations, links and sites within the fractal hierarchies of the Web while also suggesting connections between those virtual spaces and the real spaces of the urban environment, in this case a railway station in greater Tokyo. Thus, Irie's 'information scape' is a hybrid environment, a superimposition of real-world environments and virtual environments, which offers the user a multitude of interactive ways to visualize net-spaces as multilayered info-structures linked to physical environments. 'Information scapes' may be used as virtual environments for data storage, retrieval, manipulation and input. On a large scale the 'information scape' could constitute the background/stage for real-world events such as virtual studio set-ups for TV broadcasting.

Kei'ichi Irie's vision of architecture is a radical one. His Tokyo Continuum projects a scenario in which what we now call the city may disappear altogether, to be replaced by some as yet undefined virtual civitas. But perhaps Irie, an architect who also constructed several notable public buildings and private residences, is simply exploring a new space that emerges out of the fusing of the virtual and the real.

TOYO ITO
TOKYO, JAPAN

*Designing light-spaces
and 'deep-structures'
for the Digital Age*

YATSUSHIRO FIRE STATION

Oval cuts in the otherwise regular
roof plate dramatically draw the
sky into the building.

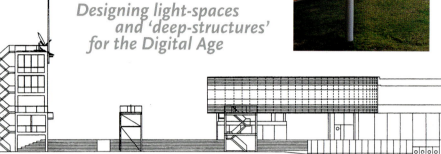

ELEVATION

YATSUSHIRO FIRE STATION

Lifted six metres off the ground, the
administration and living spaces
within the fire station are contained
in a floating plate.

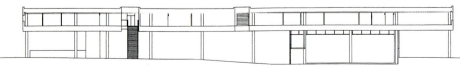

ELEVATION

TOYO ITO was one of the first architectural designers to recognize the impact of electronic media on the city and to develop the possibilities of a post-industrial architecture. He established his own office in Tokyo, producing several small buildings during the late 1970s and early to mid-1980s, which matched punched metal screens and membranes with layered translucent walls to create spaces that alluded both to Japan's traditional architecture and to the coming ephemera of the mediated city and the virtual environments of the Internet. Tellingly, in 1978 he wrote that, '… whether in buildings or in cities, we drift through a realm where symbols are drifting about and with these we weave a space of our own significance.' Ito quickly grasped the significance of Japan's technologized ascendancy and the manner in which electronic technologies were breaking down the fixed rigidities of the old city into so many floating urban metaphors. During the late 1980s he applied this understanding, creating a series of seminal nomad projects that revealed the new modes of inhabitation afforded by the new informational and urban economies. More recently as his commissions have grown larger in scale and intent, Ito has sourced the deep structures of the electronic and contemporary urban world to provide startlingly new models of inhabitation and architectural organization.

Ito's winning design for the Sendai Médiathèque, a complex containing an art gallery, a library and audio-visual facilities, combines his earlier interests in screened surfaces with an array of newer deep structures — treelike tubes that serve as integrative structural systems. The building is made up of seven square slabs of honeycombed, sandwich-panelled steel plate, which serve as

YATSUSHIRO FIRE STATION

The floating plate is punctuated by a series of oval holes that accommodate a lightweight approach staircase and deliver light and sea breezes.

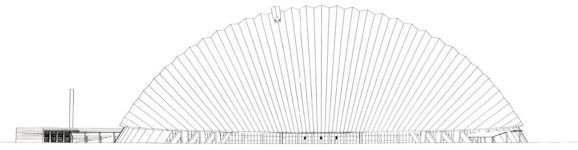

ELEVATION

O-DOME

The O-Dome in Odate is a year-round indoor baseball facility that is supported by an extremely large and complex timber structural system clad with a taut, Teflon-membraned skin.

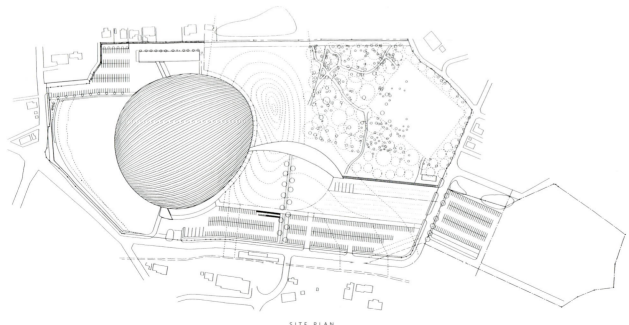

SITE PLAN

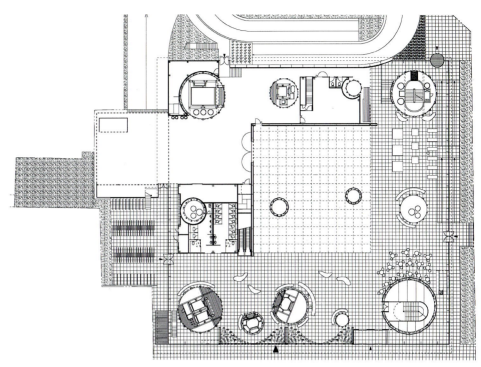

SENDAI MEDIATHEQUE

Ito's winning entry in an open
competition for a multi-use
'Médiathèque' complex combines
an art gallery, a library and audio-
visual facilities. The building weaves
slab or plate, skin and tubelike
structures into a new minimal
archetype that responds to the flows
of the electronic and natural worlds.

Unlike most closed and hospital-like aged people's homes, Ito's home for fifty elderly people is a light, almost transparent structure marked by loosely interlocked spaces.

SECOND FLOOR

floors and are hung off the tube-trees. Each tube-tree is actually a shaft formed out of a hyper-paraboloid shell made out of several slender, thick-walled tubes of steel. These pure, minimal structures serve as paths for vertical circulation and energy or information flow spaces. Wrapping these plates and tubes, the double skin creates a shimmering shroud that will cloak the project with a piece of sky.

The O-Dome in Odate, a year-round indoor baseball facility, is a far more substantial and physically evident piece of architecture that relies on an extremely large and complex timber structural system. Located in a gorge within the fertile drainage basin of the Noshiro River, the Teflon-membraned dome was designed to accommodate the wind and snow loads as well as the fluid arc of a fly ball. In situating the O-Dome, Ito chose to establish a continuum with the spacious natural environment, an overlap between the organic mood of the surrounding fields and the highly artificial, technologized spectacle-space of the baseball venue.

Toyo Ito has spoken of a 'syntax of space by collage…peculiar to Japanese culture'. In most of his projects one finds this celebration of simultaneity, somewhere at work. His projects successfully synthesize competing tendencies – fixed and fragmented space, sheer, transparent and solid planar surface treatment, traditional and contemporary references, floating and figured metaphors, organic and inorganic models – into unique compositions that reconceptualize architecture in the context of a technologically enhanced age.

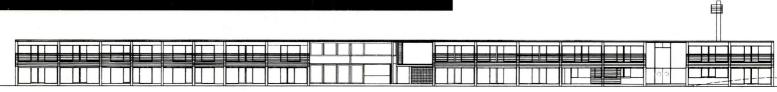

ELEVATION

ARCHITECTS' INFORMATION

ATELIER HITOSHI ABE

30-30 Takimichi, Aoba-Ku
Sendai, Miyagi 981, Japan
tel: +81 22 278 8854
fax: +81 22 277 7933

Education
PhD in Architecture, Tohku University
Master of Architecture, Southern California
    Institute of Architecture (SCIARC)
Professional Experience
Coop Himmelb(l)au

RECENT PROJECTS
A-House, Miyagi Prefecture, Japan, 1997
COMCO, relocatable, 1997
YG House, Miyagi Prefecture, Japan,
    1997
C-House, Miyagi Prefecture, Japan, 1996
Gravel 2, Miyagi Prefecture, Japan, 1996
X-Bridge, Miyagi Prefecture, Japan, 1994
XX Box, relocatable, 1993–95
Miyagi Water-Tower, Miyagi Prefecture,
    Japan, 1993–94
Shirasagi Bridge, Miyagi Prefecture,
    Japan, 1993–94
Miyagi Stadium, Miyagi Prefecture,
    Japan, 1992 to present

CLARE DESIGN

PO Box 5010, Maroochydore
South Queensland 4558, Australia
tel: +61 7 5476 8844
fax: +61 7 5476 8227

Kerry Clare
Education
Diploma in Architecture, Queensland
    University of Technology
Professional Experience
Gabriel Poole

Lindsay Clare
Education
Diploma in Architecture, Queensland
    University of Technology
Professional Experience
Gabriel Poole

RECENT PROJECTS
Cotton Tree Pilot Housing, Sunshine
    Coast, Australia, 1995
Two Houses at Noosa, Sunshine
    Coast, Australia, 1995
Hammond Residence, Sunshine
    Coast, Australia, 1994
Ski + Skurf, Sunshine Coast,
    Australia, 1994
Clare Residence, Sunshine Coast,
    Australia, 1991
Rainbow Shores, Sunshine Coast,
    Australia, 1991
McWilliam Residence, Sunshine
    Coast, Australia, 1990

DALY, GENIK

1558 10th Street
Santa Monica, CA 90405, USA
tel: +1 310 656 3180
fax: +1 310 656 3183

Kevin Daly
Education
Master of Architecture,
    Rice University
Bachelor of Arts in Architecture,
    University of California
    (Berkeley)

Professional Experience
Frank O. Gehry

Christopher Genik
Education
Master of Architecture, Rice
    University
Bachelor of Arts in Architecture,
    Carleton University
Professional Experience
Peter Waldeman

RECENT PROJECTS
Campus Cafes, Arizona State University,
    Tempe, Arizona, 1997
Mar Vista House, Los Angeles,
    California, 1996
Mooser Avakian Residence,
    Los Angeles, California, 1996
Tarzana Residence, Los Angeles,
    California, 1995

DAWSON-BROWN ARCHITECTURE

Level 1, 63 William Street
East Sydney, NSW 2010
Australia
tel: +61 2 9360 7977
fax: +61 2 9360 2123

Education
MSAAD, Columbia University
Bachelor of Architecture, University
    of New South Wales
Professional Experience
Dawson-Brown + Ackert Architecture P/L
Heritage Council
Stephenson + Turner Architects
Julian Harrap Architects

Rodney Melville & Assoc.
Canons Ashby
Caroe + Martin Architects
Fisher Lucas Architects

RECENT PROJECTS
Culburra Beach House, Culburra,
    Australia, 1997
Palm Beach House, Sydney,
    Australia, 1997
Paddington Town House, Sydney,
    Australia, 1996
Bellevue Hill Residence, Sydney,
    Australia, 1992
Brigadoon House, Perth,
    Australia, 1991

dECOi–OBJECTILE

dECOi: 65 rue du Faubourg, atelier 21,
75010 Paris, France
tel/fax: +33 1 40 22 07 03

Objectile: 25 rue Tholozé,
75018 Paris, France
tel: +33 1 46 06 87 06
fax: +33 1 46 06 19 12

Mark Goulthorpe RIBA
Education
Bachelor of Architecture,
    University of Liverpool
Student Exchange Program,
    University of Oregon
Professional Experience
Richard Meier and Partners
Walter Chatham
Mark Mack
Building Design Partnership

Yee Pin Tan
Education
Bachelor of Architecture, University
    of Oregon
History of Architecture, University
    of Pittsburgh
Professional Experience
Objectile

Patrick Beaucé
Education
Artist/Designer DNSEP (Diplôme National
    Supérieur d'Expression Plastique)
Professional Experience
Patrick Beaucé Artiste/Designeur

Bernard Cache
Education
Architecte EPFL (Ecole Poytechnique
    Fédérale de Lausanne)
Diplôme de l'Institut Polytechnique de
    Philosophie, Ecole Supérieure des
    Sciences Economiques et
    Commerciales
Professional Experience
Directeur d'études, BIPE

Taoufik Hammoudi
Education
Architecte DPLG, Ecole d'Architecture
    de Grenoble
Professional Experience
Atelier EO

RECENT PROJECTS
Eco-Taal, Manila, The Philippines,
    1997
Pallas House, Kuala Lumpur, Malaysia,
    1996–97

NEIL M. DENARI/COR-TEX
11906 Lawler Street
Los Angeles, CA 90066, USA
tel: +1 310 390 2968
fax: +1 310 390 2918

Education
Master of Architecture, Harvard
    University
Bachelor of Architecture, University
    of Houston
Professional Experience
James Stewart Polshek and Partners

RECENT PROJECTS
Tokyo HiRise, Tokyo, Japan, 1997
Vertical Smooth House, Los Angeles,
    California, 1997
Interrupted Projections Installation at
    Gallery Ma, Tokyo, Japan, 1996
National Library Kansai Division
    Competition, Seika-Cho, Kyoto
    Prefecture, Japan, 1996
Massey Residence, Los Angeles,
    California, 1994

FERNAU & HARTMAN
2512 9th Avenue #2
Berkeley, CA 94710, USA
tel: +1 510 848 4480
fax: +1 510 848 4532

Richard Fernau FAIA
Education
Master of Architecture, University of
    California (Berkeley)
Bachelor of Arts in Philosophy,
    University of California (Santa Cruz)
Professional Experience
Steiger Partner Architekten

Laura Hartman
Education
Master of Architecture, University
    of California (Berkeley)
Bachelor of Arts in Art,
    Smith College
Professional Experience
Dolf Schneibli e Associati,
    Architetti
Esherick Homsey Dodge
    and Davis

David Kau
Education
Master of Architecture, University
    of California (Berkeley)
Bachelor of Arts, Harvard University
Professional Experience
Fernau & Hartman

Annie Tilt
Education
Master of Architecture, University
    of California (Berkeley)
Bachelor of Science in Architecture and
    Engineering, Princeton University
Professional Experience
Fernau & Hartman

RECENT PROJECTS
The Steven Tipping Building, Berkeley,
    California, 1995
Westcott/Lahar House, Bolinas,
    California, 1995
Collective Housing for the Cheesecake
    Consortium, Philo, California, 1994
FX Headquarters, Los Angeles,
    California, 1994
von Stein House, Kenwood, California, 1993
Cunniff/Fernau House, Berkeley,
    California, 1992
Evergreen Valley College, San Jose,
    California, 1992
Napa Valley Museum, Yountville,
    California, 1990

FOREIGN OFFICE ARCHITECTS
Flat 2, 58 Belgrave Road
London SW1V 2BP, UK
tel: +44 171 976 5988
fax: +44 171 630 9754
email: foa@easynet.co.uk

Farshid Moussavi
Education
Master of Architecture, Harvard University
Diploma Degree in Architecture, University
    College London, Bartlett School of
    Architecture
Bachelor of Science in Architecture,
    Dundee University
Professional Experience
Office for Metropolitan Architecture
Renzo Piano Building Workshop

Alejandro Zaera Polo
Education
Master of Architecture, Harvard University
Architecture Degree with Honours, ETS,
    Madrid
Professional Experience
Office for Metropolitan Architecture

RECENT PROJECTS
National Library Kansai Division Competition,
    Seika-Cho, Kyoto Prefecture, Japan, 1996

Pusan High Speed Railway Complex,
    Pusan, South Korea, 1996
Yokohama International Ferry Terminal,
    Yokohama, Japan, 1996 to present
Meyong Dong Cathedral, Seoul,
    South Korea, 1995–96

GAS

101 Regents Park Road
London NW1 8UR, UK
tel/fax: +44 171 483 4206
email: laurence@gates.co.uk

En Loong Ng
Education
Bachelor of Science in Architecture,
    University College London, Bartlett
    School of Architecture
AA Diploma, The Architectural Association
Professional Experience
DP Architects
Jean Nouvel
BEP Sdn Bhd
T.R. Hamzah & Yeang
Conran Roach
A.R. Waller & Associates

Laurence Liauw
Education
AA Diploma, The Architectural Association
Professional Experience
Burrell Foley Fischer
Partnership with Botsford & Ceccato
T.R. Hamzah & Yeang
Partnership with Justus Pysall

Guy Westbrook
Education
AA Diploma, The Architectural Association
Bachelor of Architecture, University of
    Cape Town
Interior Design Diploma, Natal Polytechnic
Professional Experience
Battle McCarthy Engineers
Mac Architecture
Foreign Office Architects
T.R. Hamzah & Yeang
Sir Norman Foster & Partners
Areen Design

RECENT PROJECTS
C 2 Eating, Melaka, Malaysia, 1997
K Office, Subang, Malaysia, 1996
Kuala Lumpur Sub Centre (KLSC), Kuala
    Lumpur, Malaysia, 1995 to present
Optimal Form Computer-generated Solar
    Geometry Model for Malaysia, 1994

GIN + DESIGN WORKSHOP

7500A Beach Road #12-312
The Plaza, Singapore 199591
tel:+ 65 292 111
fax: +65 298 7851
email: ginarch@cyberway.com.sg

Ang Gin Wah
Education
Bachelor of Architecture, Curtin
    University of Technology, Australia
Professional Experience
Ashihara International Architect
DP Architects

RECENT PROJECTS
Wuu Apartments, Singapore, 1997
C House, Kuala Lumpur, Malaysia,
    1996–97
Ee House, Singapore, 1996
Elite Park, Singapore, 1996
Wong House, Singapore, 1994

T.R. HAMZAH & KEN YEANG

8 Jalan Satu, Taman Sri Ukay
68000 Ampang, Selangor
Malaysia
tel: +60 3 457 1966
fax: +60 3 456 1005
email: kynnet@pc.jaring.my

Ken Yeang
Education
PhD, Cambridge University
AA Diploma, The Architectural Association
Professional Experience
Own studio

RECENT PROJECTS
Gamuda Headquarters, Kuala Lumpur,
    Malaysia, 1998
Hitechniaga Tower, Kuala Lumpur,
    Malaysia, 1997
Menara UMNO Penang, Penang,
    Malaysia, 1997
Shanghai, Armoury Tower, Shanghai,
    China, 1997
Central Plaza, Kuala Lumpur, Malaysia, 1996
Maybank Chambers Tower Competition
    Entry, Boat Quay, Singapore, 1996
Menara Budaya, Kuala Lumpur,
    Malaysia, 1996
TA2, Kuala Lumpur, Malaysia
Guthrie Pavilion, Selangor, Malaysia, 1996
Menara Mesiniaga, Kuala Lumpur,
    Malaysia, 1992

KEI'ICHI IRIE/ POWER UNIT STUDIO

Daikan-yama Coop, #2107
Sarugaku-cho 12-1, Shibuya-ku
Tokyo, Japan
tel: +81 3 3461 9827
fax: +81 3 3461 9829
email: qa5k-ire@asahi-net.or.jp

Education
Master of Fine Arts, Tokyo University
Bachelor of Architecture, Tokyo
    University

Professional Experience
Power Unit Studio Co. Ltd
Irie Architects and Associates

RECENT PROJECTS
Tokyo Continuum, Japan, 1996–97
Isiuchi Dam Museum, Kumamoto
    Prefecture, Japan, 1993
Bean House, Tokyo, Japan, 1992
Caravan, Contemporary Arts Museum,
    Sydney, Australia, 1991
Prototype House in Sakurajosui,
    Tokyo, Japan, 1991
Monol, industrialized apartments,
    Prefecture, Japan, 1990

TOYO ITO

Fujiya Building, 19-4 1 Chome
Shibuya, Shibuya-ku, Tokyo 150, Japan
tel: +81 3 3409 5822
fax: +81 3 3409 5969

Education
Bachelor of Architecture, Tokyo
    University
Professional Experience
Urban Robot (URBOT)
Kiyonori Kikutake Architect
    and Associates

RECENT PROJECTS
Sendai Médiathèque, Sendai, Miyagi
    Prefecture, Japan, scheduled 2001
O Dome, Odate, Akita Prefecture, Japan,
    1997
Yatsushiro Fire Station, Yatsushiro,
    Kumamoto Prefecture, Japan, 1995
Yatsushiro Old People's Home,
    Yatsushiro, Kumamoto Prefecture,
    Japan, 1993

GLENDA KAPSTEIN

Universidad Catolica del Norte
Departmente de Arquitectura
Av. Angamos 0610
Antofagasta, Chile
tel: +56 55 241 148
fax: +56 55 241 788

Education
Master of Architecture, Catholic
    University of Santiago
Bachelor of Architecture, University
    of Chile/Valparaiso
Professional Experience
Ramón Vasquez Molezún y José
    Antonio Corrales
George Candilis

RECENT PROJECTS
Codelco Pavilion, Antofagasta,
    Chile, 1997
Retreat House, Foundation Alonso
    Ovalle, Antofagasta, Chile, 1992–95

WARO KISHI

K. Associates, 3F Yamashita Bldg
10 Koyama, Nishimotomachi
Kita-ku, Kyoto 603, Japan
fax: +81 75 492 5185
email: warox@ja2.so-net.or.jp

Education
Master of Architecture, Kyoto
University
Bachelor of Architecture, Kyoto
University
Professional Experience
Masayuki Kurokawa, Tokyo

RECENT PROJECTS
House in Higashi-nada, Kobe, Japan, 1997
House in Higashi-osaka, Osaka,
Japan,1997
Memorial Hall, Ube, Yamaguchi Prefecture,
Japan, 1997
National Library Kansai Division
Competition, Seika-Cho, Kyoto
Prefecture, Japan, 1996
Murasakino Wakuden Japanese
Restaurant, Kita-ku, Kyoto, Japan, 1995
House in Nihonbashi, Naniwa-ku,
Osaka, Japan, 1992

MATHIAS KLOTZ

Monseñor Carlos, Casa Nueva 0358
Providencia, Santiago, Chile
tel: +56 2 233 6613
fax: +56 2 232 3282

Education
Bachelor of Architecture, Catholic
University of Chile/Santiago
Professional Experience
Mathias Klotz Germain Architect

RECENT PROJECTS
Edificio Pizzaras Ibérnicas, Huechuraba,
Region Metropolitana, Chile, 1997
Casa Klotz, Playa Grande de
Tongoy, Chile, 1995
Casa Ugarte, Manticillo Sur, Chile, 1995
Casa Müller, Isla Grande de Chiloé,
X Region, Chile, 1994

KNTA

1154A Rochor Road
Singapore 188429
tel: +65 336 7228
fax: +65 336 7310
email: kntals@singnet.com.sg

Kay Ngee Tan
Education
AA Diploma, The Architectural
Association
Professional Experience
Arup Associates, London
Studio Tomassini, Milan

Tan Teck Kiam
Education
Bachelor of Architecture, National
University of Singapore
Postgraduate studies, University
College London
Professional Experience
William Lim Associates

RECENT PROJECTS
Check's House 2, Cluny Park,
Singapore, 1998
1 Corfe Place, Corfe Place, Singapore, 1997
Dyson House, Dyson Road, Singapore, 1997
Emerald Hill House, Emerald Hill Road,
Singapore, 1997
Federation Square Competition Entry,
Melbourne, Australia, 1997
Kitokuniya Bangkok, Bangkok,
Thailand, 1997
Three houses, Nassim Road,
Singapore, 1997
15 Alnwick Road, Alnwick Road,
Singapore, 1996
Kitokuniya Sydney, Sydney, Australia, 1996
Maybank Chambers Tower Competition
Entry, Boat Quay, Singapore, 1996
Page One Kuala Lumpur, Kuala Lumpur,
Malaysia, 1996
Shude Housing, Shude, Guangzhou,
China, 1996
Page One Melbourne, Melbourne,
Australia, 1995
Check's House 1, Cluny Park, Singapore, 1993

LEGORRETA ARQUITECTOS

Palacio de Versailles 285 "A"
Mexico City DF, 11020 Mexico
tel: +52 5 251 96 98
fax: +52 5 596 61 62

Ricardo Legorreta Hon. FAIA
Education
Bachelor of Architecture, Universidad
Nacional Autonoma de Mexico
Professional Experience
José Villagran García

Victor Legorreta
Education
Bachelor of Architecture, Universidad
Iberoamericana, Mexico City
Professional Experience
Fumihiko Maki
Martorell, Bohigas and Mackay

RECENT PROJECTS
Monterrey Central Library, San Nicolás de
los Garza, Nuevo León, Mexico, 1994
Metropolitan Cathedral Managua,
Managua, Nicaragua, 1993
MARCO Contemporary Art Museum,
Monterrey, Nuevo León, Mexico, 1991
Rancho Santa Fe House, Rancho Santa Fe,
California, 1987

LYON ARCHITECTS

Level 3, 470 Collins Street
Melbourne, Victoria 3000, Australia
tel: +61 3 9614 5866
fax: +61 3 9614 5877

Carey Lyon
Education
Master of Architecture, RMIT University
Bachelor of Architecture, University of
Melbourne
Professional Experience
Perrott Lyon Mathieson Pty Ltd

RECENT PROJECTS
RMIT University Swanston Sports Health
and Education Building, Melbourne,
Australia, scheduled 2000
Lilydale Lake Campus Eastern Institute
of TAFE, Lilydale, Australia, 1998
New Benalla Campus, Goulburn Ovens
Institute of TAFE, Benalla, Australia,
1998
Box Hill Institute of TAFE, Nelson
Campus, Stage Two, Melbourne,
Australia, 1997
Federation Square Competition Entry,
Melbourne, Australia, 1997
Pacific Central Development Competition
Entry, Melbourne, Australia, 1996
Box Hill Institute of TAFE Nelson Campus
Stage One, Melbourne, Australia, 1995
Sunshine Campus Western Hospital Institute
of TAFE, Melbourne, Australia, 1994
The Edmund Barton Centre, Barton Institute
of TAFE, Melbourne, Australia, 1993

MIKAN

Tamagawa 2-17-14
Setagaya-ku, 158 Tokyo, Japan
tel: +81 3 3707 7820
fax: +81 3 3707 7819
email: kinkan@po.iijnet.or.jp

Kiwako Kamo
Education
Master of Architecture, Tokyo Institute
of Technology
Professional Experience
Célavi Associates
Kume and Partners

Yosuke Kumakura
Education
PhD, Tokyo Metropolitan University
Professional Experience
Yosuke Kumakura Architect

Masashi Sogabe
Education
Master of Architecture, Tokyo Institute
of Technology
Professional Experience
Sogabe Atelier
Toyo Ito Associates

Masayoshi Takeuchi
Education
Master of Architecture, Tokyo
  Institute of Technology
Professional Experience
Atelier Takeuchi
Work Station

Manuel Tardits
Education
PhD and Master of Architecture,
  University of Tokyo
Architecte DPLG, Unité Pédagogique
  d'Architecture n°1, Paris
Professional Experience
Célavi Associates

RECENT PROJECTS
Kanban, Koban (Police Box) by Célavi
  Associates, Kumamoto, Japan, 1997
Nagano NHK Broadcasting Station
  by Mikan, Nagano, Japan, 1997
Kirishima Art Hall by Mikan, Kirashima,
  Japan, 1996
Kugayama Annex by Atelier Takeuchi,
  Tokyo, Japan, 1995

MILLER/HULL
PARTNERSHIP
Maritime Building,
911 Western Avenue, Room 220
Seattle, WA 98104-1031, USA
tel: +1 206 682 6837
fax: +1 206 682 5692

David E. Miller FAIA
Education
Master of Architecture, University
  of Illinois
Bachelor of Architecture, Washington
  State University
Professional Experience
RIA Architects
Arthur Erickson Architects
Skidmore Owings and Merril
US Peace Corps in Brazil

Robert E. Hull FAIA
Education
Bachelor of Architecture, Washington
  State University
Professional Experience
RIA Architects
Marcel Breuer, New York
US Peace Corps in Afghanistan

Craig A. Curtis
Education
Bachelor of Science in Construction
  Management,Washington State
  University
Bachelor of Architecture, Washington
  State University
Professional Experience
Austin Hansen Feldman Group

Norm H. Strong
Education
Bachelor of Architecture,
  Washington State University
Bachelor of Science in Architectural
  Studies, Washington State University
Professional Experience
Miller/Hull Partnership

Steven B. Tatge
Education
Master of Architecture, University
  of Washington
Bachelor of Psychology, Knox University
Professional Experience
NBBJ Group
Hamilton Architects

Amy H. Lelyveld
Education
Master of Architecture, Yale University
Bachelor of Arts, University of
  Chicago
Professional Experience
Sriris/Coombs Architects
Yale Construction Management
Richard Gluckman Architects

Scott A. Wolf
Education
Master of Architecture, University
  of Oregon
Bachelor of Environmental Design in
  Architecture, North Carolina State
  University
Professional Experience
Rex Hohlbein Architects
Hamilton Architects
Notter, Finegold and Alexander
SWA Architects

RECENT PROJECTS
Point Roberts Border Station,
  Point Roberts, Washington, 1997
NW Federal Credit Union, Seattle,
  Washington, 1996
Garfield Community Center, Seattle,
  Washington, 1995
Island Cabin, Decatur Island,
  Washington, 1995
Olympic College Shelton, Shelton,
  Washington, 1995
Marquand Retreat, Yakima,
  Washington, 1992

MORPHOSIS ARCHITECTS
2041 Colorado Avenue
Santa Monica, CA 90405, USA
tel: +1 310 453 2247
fax: +1 310 829 327
email: morphosis@earthlink.net

Thom Mayne FAIA
Education
Master of Architecture, Harvard University

Bachelor of Architecture, University
  of Southern California
Professional Experience
Victor Gruen

RECENT PROJECTS
ASE Taipei Design Center, Hsichih,
  Taiwan, 1995–97
Sun Tower, Seoul, South Korea, 1995–97
Blades Residence, Santa Barbara,
  California, 1991–97

ERIC OWEN MOSS
8557 Higuera Street
Culver City, CA 90232, USA
tel: +1 310 839 1199
fax: +1 310 839 7922
email: ericowenmoss@juno.com

Education
Master of Architecture, Harvard University
Bachelor of Architecture, University of
  California (Berkeley)
Professional Experience
Own studio

RECENT PROJECTS
Bee Hive, Culver City, California, 1997
Pittard Sullivan, Culver City, California,
  1997
Stealth, Culver City, California, 1996
Samitaur, Culver City, California, 1995
The Box , Culver City, California, 1994

HIROSHI NAITO
#301 Matsuoka Kudan Building
2-2-8-301, Kudan-minami
Chiyoda-ku, Tokyo 102, Japan
tel: +81 3 3262 9636
fax: +81 3 3262 9804

Education
Master of Architecture, Waseda University
Bachelor of Architecture, Waseda University
Professional Experience
Kiyonori Kikutake Architect and Associates
Fernand Higueras

RECENT PROJECTS
Chihiro Art Museum, Azumino,
  Matsukawamura, Nagano Prefecture,
  Japan, 1997
Shima Art Museum, Toba, Mie Prefecture,
  Japan, 1993
Sea Folk Museum, Toba, Mie Prefecture,
  Japan, 1992

ROB WELLINGTON
QUIGLEY
434 West Cedar Street
San Diego, CA 92001, USA
tel: +1 619 232 0888
fax: +1 619 232 8966

Education
Bachelor of Architecture, University of Utah
Professional Experience
Gluth and Quigley Architecture
US Peace Corps in Chile

RECENT PROJECTS
Shaw Lopez Ridge, San Diego,
    California, 1996
Solana Beach Transit Station, Solana
    Beach, California, 1995
Esperanza Gardens Apartments,
    Encinitas, California, 1994
Sherman Heights Community Center,
    San Diego, California, 1994
Capistrano Beach House, Capistrano
    Beach, California, 1993
202 Island Inn, San Diego, California, 1992
Linda Vista Library, San Diego,
    California, 1987

TAX (Taller Arquitectura X)
Atlanta 143, col. Nochebuena CP
Mexico City DF, 03720 Mexico
tel: +52 5 611 1771
fax: +52 5 598 5431

Daniel Alvarez + Alberto Kalach
Education
Universidad Iberoamericana, Mexico City
Cornell University
Professional Experience
Own studio

RECENT PROJECTS
Maguen David Community Center,
    Cuajimalpa, state of Mexico,
    Mexico, 1997
Negro House, Mexico City, Mexico, 1997
The Alexander von Humboldt German
    School in Puebla, Puebla, Mexico, 1997
Adolf Building, Mexico City, Mexico, 1996
House in Valle de Bravo, Valle de Bravo,
    Mexico, 1994

TEN ARQUITECTOS
C/ Cuernavaca 114,
PB Colonia Condensa
Mexico City DF, 06140 Mexico
tel: +52 5 286 00 74
fax: +52 5 286 17 35
email: tenarq@mail.internet.com.mx

Enrique Norten
Education
Master of Architecture, Cornell
    University
Bachelor of Architecture, Universidad
    Iberoamericana, Mexico City
Professional Experience
Enrique Norten Arquitecto
Albin y Norten Arquitectos
Boris Albin
Abraham Zabludovsky

Bernardo Gomez-Pimienta
Education
Master of Architecture, Columbia University
Bachelor of Architecture, Universidad
    Anahuac, Mexico CIty
Professional Experience
VISUAL International
George Wimpey

RECENT PROJECTS
Museum of Sciences, Mexico City,
    Mexico, 1997
House LE, Mexico City, Mexico, 1995
Drama Centre, Mexico City, Mexico, 1994

KERSTIN THOMPSON ARCHITECTS
96 Webb Street, Fitzroy
Victoria 3065, Australia
tel: +61 3 9419 4969
fax: +61 3 9419 4483

Education
Bachelor of Architecture, RMIT
Professional Experience
BTH
Perrott Lyon Mathieson Pty Ltd
Robinson Chen Pty Ltd
Matteo Thun, Milan

RECENT PROJECTS
Amess Street, Melbourne,
    Australia, 1998
Howe Crescent, Melbourne,
    Australia, 1998
Skenes Creek House, Skenes Creek,
    Australia, 1998
Tarrawarra Vineyard, Yarraglen,
    Australia, 1998
Barkers Creek House, Castlemaine,
    Australia, 1996
Webb Street Residence, Melbourne,
    Australia, 1995
Morgan House, Lorne, Australia, 1992

MICHAEL TONKIN ARCHITECTURE AND DESIGN
5F/ Wah Hing Bldg, 35 Pottinger Street
Central, Hong Kong
tel: +852 2869 6311
fax: +852 2574 3905
email: tonkin@asiaonline.net

Education
Master of Arts in Architecture & Design
    Studies, Royal College of Art, London
Bachelor of Arts in Architecture, Leeds
    School of Architecture
Professional Experience
Tonkin Architect, London
Eva Jiricna Architects
Branson Coates Architecture
Rock Townsend

RECENT PROJECTS
Flex Bar, Central, Hong Kong, 1997
Font Works, Tsim Sha Tsui,
    Hong Kong, 1997
Stanley House, Stanley,
    Hong Kong, 1997
Broadway Yuen Long Cinema,
    New Territories, Hong Kong, 1996
Oscars Restaurant, Causeway Bay,
    Hong Kong, 1995
Q Restaurant, Quarry Bay,
    Hong Kong, 1995
Ubud Hotel, Bali, Indonesia, 1994

USHIDA FINDLAY PARTNERSHIP
402, 5-12-15 Kitashinagawa
Shinagawa-ku, Tokyo 141, Japan
tel: +81 3 3440 4609
fax: +81 3 3444 6907
email: ufp@a1.mbn.or.jp

Eisaku Ushida
Education
Bachelor of Architecture, University
    of Tokyo
Professional Experience
Arata Isozaki and Associates
Richard Rogers Partnership

Kathryn Findlay RIBA
Education
AA Diploma, The Architectural
    Association
Postgraduate Research, University
    of Tokyo
Professional Experience
Arata Isozaki and Associates

RECENT PROJECTS
Federation Square Competition Entry,
    Melbourne, Australia, 1997
Polyphony House, Osaka, Japan, 1997
Parallel Landscapes Installation at
    Gallery Ma, Tokyo, Japan, 1996
S Project, Tokyo, Japan, 1995
Kaizankyo, Wakayama Prefecture, Japan, 1994
Soft and Hairy House, Tsukuba New
    Science City, Japan, 1993
Truss Wall House, Tokyo, Japan, 1993
Echo Chamber, Tokyo, Japan, 1989

STEPHEN VARADY
363a Pitt Street, Sydney
NSW 2000, Australia
tel: +61 2 9283 6880
fax: +61 2 9283 6886

Education
Bachelor of Architecture, University
    of New South Wales
Professional Experience
George Freedman Associates
Phillip Cox

RECENT PROJECTS

Circular Quay Urban Design
   Competition, Sydney, Australia, 1995
Manning Residence, Paddington,
   Australia, 1995
Measday Residence, Woollahra,
   Australia, 1994
Slobam/Parham Residence,
   Melbourne, Australia, 1994
Perraton Apartment, Sydney,
   Australia, 1992

ARCHITECTURE WARREN & MAHONEY

131 Victoria Street
PO Box 25086
Christchurch, New Zealand
tel: +64 3 961 5926
fax: +64 3 961 5935

Thom Craig
Education
Bachelor of Architecture, University
   of Natal, Durban
Professional Experience
Barclay Architects, Christchurch
Jan van Wijk
Luis Ferreira da Silva, Bruce Stafford
   and Andre Hodgskin
Willie Meyre & François Pienaar
   Architects
Bannie Britz & Michael Scholes
   Architects
Ing Jackson DeRavel & Hartley

Barry Dacombe
Education
Bachelor of Architecture, University
   of Auckland
Professional Experience
Architecture Warren & Mahoney

Kerry Mason
Education
Extramural Qualification, University
   of Auckland

New Zealand Certificate of Drafting
   (Architecture), Christchurch
   Polytechnic
Certificate of Design (Architecture),
   British Columbia Institute of Technology
Professional Experience
Hawthorn Mansfield Architects

Steve McCraken
Education
Bachelor of Architecture,
   University of Auckland
Professional Experience
Salmon and Burt
Mason and Wales
Ministry of Works
Yakeley Associates
Davis Heather Group

Bren Morrison
Education
Bachelor of Architecture,
   University of Auckland
Professional Experience
Mason and Wales
M.J. Cockburn Group Planners
Gillespie Newman Pierce
R.G. Herriot

Roy Wilson
Education
Bachelor of Architecture,
   University of Auckland
Professional Experience
Ketley, Could and Clark
Gillespie Newman Pierce
Cutter Pickmere Douglas
Peter Bevan

RECENT PROJECTS

Architecture Warren & Mahoney office,
   Christchurch, New Zealand, 1997
Christchurch Convention Centre,
   Christchurch, New Zealand, 1997
O'Connell House, Christchurch,
   New Zealand, 1996
House Carr, Christchurch,

New Zealand, 1995
Miramar Golfcourse Clubhouse,
   Wellington, New Zealand, 1995
Christchurch Railway Station,
   Christchurch, New Zealand, 1993

KYU SUNG WOO ARCHITECTS

488 Green Street
Cambridge, MA 02139, USA
tel: +1 617 547 0128
fax: +1 617 547 9675
email: kswa@kswa.com

Education
Master of Architecture in Urban Design,
   Graduate School of Design,
   Harvard University
Master of Science in Architecture,
   School of Architecture,
   Columbia University
Master of Science in Architectural
   Engineering, Seoul National
   University
Bachelor of Science in Architectural
   Engineering, Seoul National
   University
Professional Experience
Woo and Williams
Senior Urban Designer, Mayor's Office
   of Midtown Planning and Development,
   City of New York
Urban Design Consultant, Harbison
   New Towne
Sert, Jackson & Associates
The Housing, Urban and Regional
   Planning Institute, Korean Ministry
   of Construction

RECENT PROJECTS

Stone Cloud House, Seoul, South Korea,
   1996
Whanki Museum, Seoul, 1988–94
Athletes' and Reporters' Village, Games
   of the XXIV Olympiad, Seoul,
   South Korea, 1988

BIBLIOGRAPHY

Trevor Boddy, "Vancouver's Vital Signs" in *Architecture*, New York: September 1996

David Clark, *Urban World/Global City*, London: Routledge 1996

William J.R. Curtis, *Modern Architecture Since 1990*, London: Phaidon Press 1996 (3rd edn)

William J.R. Curtis, " Mythical Landscapes: Modern Architecture and the Mexican Past" in Alicia Azuela, ed., *Hechizo de Oaxaca*, Monterrey 1991

Mike Davis, *City of Quartz- Excavating the Future in Los Angeles*, New York: Random House 1992

John Eade (ed.), *Living the Global City: Globalization as Local Process*, London: Routledge 1997

Umberto Eco, *Travels in Hyperreality*, London: Picador 1987 (2nd edn)

Kenneth Frampton, "Critical Regionalism: Modern Architecture and Cultural Identity" in *Modern Architecture: A Critical History*, London: Thames and Hudson 1992 (3rd edn)

William Gibson, *Neuromancer*, New York: Ace 1984

Rem Koolhaas, *S, M, L, XL*, Rotterdam: 010 Publishers 1995

Kenichi Ohmae, *The Borderless World: Power and Strategy in the Interlinked Economy*, New York: Harper 1990

Rodrigo Pérez de Arce, "Chile: so far yet so near" in *Abitare*, no. 353, Milan: July 1996

David Reid (ed.), *Sex, Death and God in L.A.*, Berkeley: University of California Press 1994

Peter G. Rowe, "Modern and Asian" in *Harvard Design Magazine*, Cambridge: Harvard GSD Press 1996, Winter/Spring 1997, pp 30–35

Saskia Sassen, *Cities in a World Economy*, Thousand Oaks: Pine Forge Press 1994

Deyan Sudjic, "The East is Big" in *Blueprint*, no. 116, London: Wordsearch Ltd April 1995

Jennifer Taylor, "Australian Architecture and the Imprint of Colonisation" in *Space Design*, no. 9604, Tokyo: March 1996

Debora Vrana, "Classic southland homes, just 9000 miles from Downtown L.A." in *Los Angeles Times*, 7 January 1996

Rob Wilson and Arif Dirlik(eds) *Asia/Pacific as Space of Cultural Production*, Durham: Duke University Press 1995

Rob Wilson and Wimal Dissanayake (eds) *Global/Local: Cultural Production and the Transnational Imaginary*, Durham: Duke University Press 1996

PHOTOGRAPHY CREDITS

ATELIER HITOSHI ABE
Atelier Hitoshi Abe: all photos

CLARE DESIGN
Reiner Blunck: Clare, Hammond Residences; *Adrian Boddy*: Ski + Skurf; *Richard Stringer*: McWilliam Residence, Cotton Tree, Rainbow Shores

DALY, GENIK
Scott Smith: Mooser Avakian Residence; *Dominique Vorillion*: Tarzana Residence

DAWSON-BROWN ARCHITECTURE
Robert Dawson-Brown: Paddington Townhouse, Palm Beach House; *Sharrin Rees*: Bellevue Hill Residence

NEIL M. DENARI/COR-TEX
Fujitsuka Mitsumasa: all photos

FERNAU & HARTMAN
Richard Barnes: von Stein House, Cunniff/Fernau House, Collective Housing for the Cheesecake Consortium, The Steven Tipping Building; *Cesar Rubio*: Westcott/Lahar House

GAS
GAS: all photos

GIN+DESIGN WORKSHOP
Satoshi Asakawa: all photos

T.R. HAMZAH & YEANG
T.R. Hamzah & Yeang: all photos

TOYO ITO
Naoya Hatakeyama: Old People's Home in Yatsushiro, Yatsushiro Fire Station, Sendai Médiathèque; *Mikio Kamaya*: O Dome in Odate

GLENDA KAPSTEIN
Glenda Kapstein: all photos

WARO KISHI
Hiroyuki Hirai: all photos

MATHIAS KLOTZ
Alberto Piovano: all photos

KNTA
Dennis Gilbert: Check's House 1; *KNTA*: all other projects

LEGORRETA ARQUITECTOS
Lourdes Legorreta: all photos

LYON ARCHITECTS
Carey Lyon: all photos

MIKAN
Shigeru Hiraga: NHK, Kugayama Annex, Kirishima Art Hall

MILLER/HULL PARTNERSHIP
Chris Eden: Island Cabin, Olympic College (south elevation); *Robert Hull*: Olympic College (all others); *David Miller*: Marquand Retreat

MORPHOSIS
Kim Zwarts Photography: Blades Residence; *Chou Yu-Hsien Studio*: ASE Design Centre; *IL Associates*: Sun Tower

ERIC OWEN MOSS
Thomas Bonner: Samitaur, the Box, Pittard Sullivan; *Todd Conversano*: Stealth

HIROSHI NAITO
Hiroshi Naito: all photos

ROB WELLINGTON QUIGLEY
Rob Wellington Quigley: Shaw Lopez Ridge, Esperanza Gardens Apartments, Sherman Heights Community Center, Capistrano Beach House, Solana Beach Transit Station, 202 Island Inn;

Hewitt/Garrison: Esperanza Gardens Apartments, Sherman Heights Community Center, Capistrano Beach House

TAX
Paul Czitrom: all photos

TEN ARQUITECTOS
Luis Gordoa: all photos

KERSTIN THOMPSON ARCHITECTS
Trevor Mein: Morgan House

MICHAEL TONKIN ARCHITECTURE AND DESIGN
Jonathan Pile: Q Bar, Stanley House; *Andrew Wood*: Oscars, Q Bar; *Freeman Wong*: Fontworks, Oscars; *Jane McLennan/Lily Wong*: Q Bar; *Tim McDowell*: Stanley House

USHIDA FINDLAY PARTNERSHIP
Katsuhisa Kida: all photos

STEPHEN VARADY
Stephen Varady: all photos

ARCHITECTURE WARREN & MAHONEY
Juliet Nichols: House Carr; *Euon Sarginson*, Studio La Gonda: O'Connell House; *Maurice Mahoney*: Christchurch Railway Station

KYU SUNG WOO
Timothy Hursley: Stone Cloud House, Whanki Museum; *Kyu Sung Woo*: Athletes' and Reporters' Village